The Middle Age

LONGMAN SECONDARY HISTORIES

R. J. Cootes and L. E. Snellgrove

The Middle Ages

R. J. COOTES

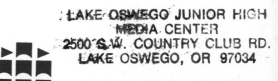

LONGMAN

LONGMAN GROUP LIMITED
Longman House, Burnt Mill, Harlow,
Essex CM20 2JE, England
and Associated Companies throughout the World.

First published 1972
Eleventh impression 1984

ISBN 0 582 20510 7

Printed in Hong Kong by
Sheck Wah Tong Printing Press Ltd.

Contents

Acknowledgements

The author and publisher are grateful to the following for permission to reproduce photographs:

Aerofilms Ltd. 29, 94, 95, 118, 133, 136, 146, 147; The Ashmolean Museum 26/27, 34/35; Barnaby's Picture Library 12, 18, 117; BBC Hulton Picture Library, 51; Bibliothéque Nationale, Paris 48; The Bodleian Library 24, 108/9; British Museum 3, 10 (above), 17 (above), 18/19, 25, 27, 28, 32, 34/35, 59 (above), 71, 97, 100, 104, 105, 106, 109, 112, 115, 126/127, 135, 138, 141, 156 (below), 157, 161 (above right and below), 167, 168/9, 172, 173, 176 (above), 177, 180, 181, 188, 189, 190, 191; British Tourist Authority 174; Cambridge University Library 186/7; Camera Press 40, 44; J. Allan Cash 39, 40/41; Central Office of Information 153; Contemporary Films Ltd, 11; Corpus Christi College, Oxford 91; The Dean and Chapter of Durham Cathedral 110; Department of the Environment, British Crown copyright 192; The Syndics of the Fitzwilliam Museum Cambridge 101; Foto Enit Rome 12/13; John R. Freeman 73, 74, 75, 76 (left), 77, 78/79, 80/81; French Government Tourist Office 121, 183; The Friends of Canterbury Cathedral 110/11; Deutsches Ledermuseum, Offenbach/Main 154; Giraudon 14, 16, 17 (below), 113, 124; Grand National Archery Society 176 (below); The Hunterian Museum Glasgow 144/5; Huntington Library, San Marino, California 142/3; The Ipswich Museum Committee 2/3; Dr. J. K. St. Joseph 62/3; A. F. Kersting 20/21, 55, 64/65, 88, 92, 114, 175; Keystone Press Agency 13; Mansell Collection 6/7, 10 (below), 14/15, 72, 86, 108, 119, 125, 130/131, 179, 187, 188/9; Mansell/Giraudon 47; Metropolitan Museum of Art gift of George Blumenthal 1941, 54; Ministry of Public Building and Works 88, 149, 151, 158/159; National Monuments Record 102, 103, 132/133, 148, 150 (below), 156(above); National Museum Copenhagen Denmark 60; National Portrait Gallery 83, 182, 186; Photohaus Zumbühl 49; Picturepoint Ltd. 41, 45, 120; Museum for Prehistoric Archaeology of Schleswig-Holstein 5; Press Association 192/193; Public Record Office 90/91; Rev. M. Ridgeway, Church of St. Michael, Beetham 132; Royal Dutch Ministry for Foreign Affairs 59 (below); Bibliotheque Royale Albert I, Bruxelles, 166/167; Scala 37, 161 (above left); The Scotsman 22; Photo: Science Museum London 76 (right), 162; Staatsbibliothek Bamberg, 48; Lawrence Stone (Courtauld Institute negative) 122/3; St. John Ambulance 117 (below); The Master and Fellows of Trinity College, Cambridge 98, 99, 166; The Board of Trinity College Dublin 156 (below); Universitet ets Oldsaksamling, Oslo 56; Victoria and Albert Museum 154/155; Babara Wagstaff 2; Warburg Institute 128; The Dean and Chapter of Westminster Abbey 150 (above). Reproduced by Gracious Permission of Her Majesty the Queen. (Royal Library, Windsor Castle), 129.

Preface

This book has been designed chiefly for pupils aged about twelve or thirteen. Great care has been taken to keep the language clear and simple. As an aid to clarity, and in the hope of stimulating some genuine interest and understanding, major topics are given a more generous allocation of space than is customary in books of this kind. It is felt that most pupils derive little benefit from a brief, superficial coverage of history.

Some topics often treated separately, including castles, methods of warfare and the development of the legal system, are here incorporated into chapters with a chronological framework. It is felt that, where possible, social and political aspects should be integrated, to offer the reader 'pegs' to hang things on.

English history provides the backbone of the book, but major European and Near-Eastern events and personalities have not been ignored. Thus almost half the chapters are devoted either wholly or partly to developments outside England.

At best, general 'textbooks' are a springboard for more thorough study. Consequently this book is offered not as a course in itself but as a *focus* for a course, giving shape and direction to pupils' studies. It is assumed that teachers will want to use all kinds of additional material with their classes, and to this end it is hoped that the '*More about* . . .' sections following each chapter will prove helpful—not only to teachers but to pupils engaged on independent assignments. Simplicity of style and language were taken into account when compiling the book lists. As a rule an attempt has been made to include material of varying degrees of difficulty. The same is true of the suggestions for written work. Most of these have been tried and tested with pupils in this age group.

I should like to thank Dr Marjorie Reeves, Mr L. E. Snellgrove, and my wife for their advice and encouragement.

RICHARD J. COOTES

To the Reader

'The Middle Ages' and 'Medieval'

In studying history it is useful to divide the past into large chunks or 'periods' of time. No doubt you have already come across such terms as *The Ancient World* or *Ancient Times*—the oldest period of man's history, ending with the break-up of the Roman Empire. At the other end of the scale, we call the most recent period of history—the last four or five hundred years—*The Modern Age*.

It follows that the years in between ancient and modern history are called *The Middle Ages,* or *Medieval Times* (the Latin for Middle Age is *medium aevum,* and from this we get the word medieval). But of course men and women living then did not think of themselves as 'medieval people'! Each man's own lifetime is, to him, the latest age. Remember that all such periods of history were invented long afterwards by scholars looking back at the past.

In this series of books the Middle Ages is taken to be roughly a thousand years, from the fifth century to the fifteenth. Some other books have slightly different divisions of time. But this is not important—the people, events and dates remain the same no matter which 'period' they are put in!

Note on the use of italics

Many teachers encourage pupils to build up their own glossaries of unfamiliar or foreign words and specialist or 'technical' terms relating to each historical period. To make this task easier, such words have been printed in *italics* at the point where they are explained in the text.

1 The Coming of the English

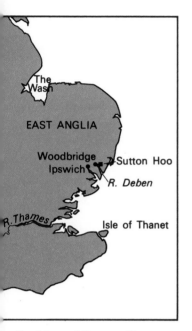

Position of Sutton Hoo

On Monday, May 8, I arrived at Sutton Hoo . . . upon my asking Mrs Pretty which mound she would like opened, she pointed to the largest of the group and said: 'What about this?' and I replied that it would be quite all right for me.

These words were written in 1939 by Mr Basil Brown, an archaeologist from Ipswich Museum. Little did he know that this brief conversation was to lead to the discovery of one of the richest treasures ever dug from British soil!

Mrs Edith Pretty was a Suffolk Landowner. She had invited archaeologists to come and dig in the grounds of her estate, at Sutton Hoo, near Woodbridge. On sandy heathland alongside the estuary of the River Deben there was a group of eleven *barrows—* earth mounds, which ancient peoples piled over the graves of the dead. (Recently much grass and bracken has been cleared and five more barrows can be seen.) Such burial mounds are quite common in Britain, but Mrs Pretty had a feeling that the ones on her estate might contain something out of the ordinary.

Treasure at Sutton Hoo

Three of the smaller barrows had been opened by Mr Brown on a previous visit in 1938. One contained traces of a small wooden boat, but the mound had been broken into by robbers and little else was left. Another mound held remains of two cremated bodies and a few objects of glass, bronze and stone. These early finds were a little disappointing. However, Mrs Pretty was determined not to give up, at least until the highest of the barrows had been opened. So in May 1939, Mr Brown resumed his diggings.

'The first find was a loose ship-nail and then five others in position', he wrote. 'We were definitely at one end of a ship.' The timber had rotted away, but the iron nails could still be seen and the decayed planks left a dark smear in the sandy soil. When the earth was scraped out the imprint of a large rowing galley was clearly revealed. It was about eighty feet long and there were places for thirty-eight oarsmen.

This was an exciting discovery. However, by June it seemed that there might be much more than just traces of a ship. Work was stopped and, early in July, a team of top experts from the British Museum and Office of Works took control of the site. Already rumours were beginning to spread, so a police guard had to be provided.

Before long a collapsed burial chamber was found in the centre of the ship. Gently removing the soil with paintbrushes, the archaeologists uncovered a priceless treasure which had lain there for about 1,300 years. There were rare and beautiful pieces of English

The barrow containing the treasure ship pictured before the 'dig' began

The Sutton Hoo ship imprint uncovered

This helmet was reconstructed out of hundreds of crumbling fragments found in the burial chamber of the Sutton Hoo ship. It took six months of continuous work to piece it together

jewellery; fragments of a six-stringed musical instrument; gold coins from Gaul (France); silver spoons and bowls from as far away as Egypt and the eastern Mediterranean lands; a coat of chain-mail, rusted into a solid mass; a helmet, shield and sword from Sweden, and many other precious objects. They help us to date the burial at about A.D. 640.

Great care was needed in removing the finds, because most of them were in a very delicate condition. This work was finished only a few days before the outbreak of the Second World War (3 September 1939). According to the law, everything belonged to Mrs Pretty, but with great generosity she decided to give her treasure to the nation. It was taken to the British Museum in London, where it can be seen today.

Meanwhile, historians began trying to explain these strange and wonderful discoveries. Without doubt the ship was buried by people known as the Anglo-Saxons—the first 'Englishmen'. We cannot be sure, but most experts think the burial was in honour of a royal person. The pagan custom of putting a dead king in a ship with his treasure beside him was later described in an Old English poem called *Beowulf:* 'They set down their dear king amidships, close by the mast. A mass of treasure was brought there from distant parts. No ship, they say, was ever so well equipped with swords, weapons and armour.'

But there is an unsolved mystery about Sutton Hoo. The ship contained no trace of a human body! Thus it was probably a memorial rather than a grave. Some historians have connected it with a local king of East Anglia called Ethelhere, who died in a battle in northern England in 654. Many of the warriors that day were swept away by a river in flood. This might explain the empty tomb. Perhaps Ethelhere's subjects believed his spirit would return to the ship, so they buried the things they thought he would need on his voyage to the after-world.

Who were the English?

The Anglo-Saxons, or English, came from the continent of Europe and began settling in Britain about 200 years before the time of the Sutton Hoo burial. Their coming was a result of the collapse of the great Roman Empire which, up to about A.D. 400, covered most of the known world, including Britain. The English settlements were

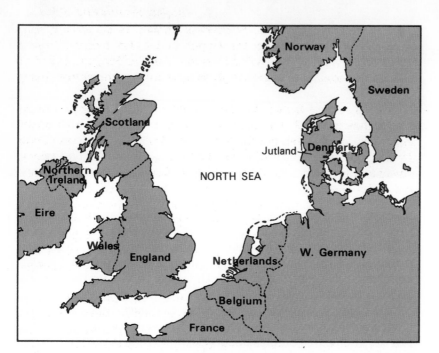

The present-day countries of north-western Europe

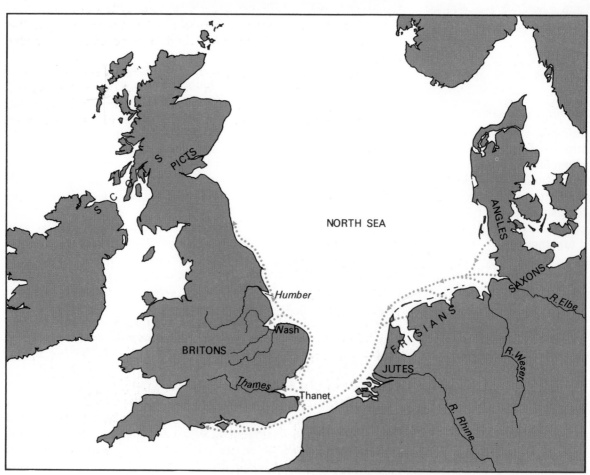

North-western Europe in the fifth century: the homelands of the English invaders

part of a great movement of peoples known as *barbarians,* who invaded the western half of the Empire in the fifth century. To us a barbarian is a brutal, uncivilised person. But the Romans called all foreigners barbarians, even though many of them were far from being savages.

The Romans in Britain had been threatened by barbarian attacks long before they left the country—in about 410. Their well-drilled legions fought to keep out the fierce Picts from the North; the Scots (then living in Ireland) who attacked the west coasts, and raiders called Saxons from across the North Sea. But when the legions were ordered back to Italy the Britons had to defend themselves.

The Saxons and other seafaring peoples from the Continent saw their chance. At first they had come for plunder; carrying away corn, weapons and slaves. But after the Roman legions had gone, they turned from piracy to full-scale invasion. The fertile soil and mild climate of Britain must have been very inviting to these tribes from the bleak, windswept lands of northern Europe.

The Romans, and many earlier peoples, left written records of their history. But hardly any barbarians could read or write. Thus the threads of history are difficult to unravel in the next few centuries after the fall of the Roman Empire. We call this period the 'Dark Ages' because so little is known about it. Historians have to work like detectives, piecing together a story from a few scattered clues. This explains why the Sutton Hoo burial was such an exciting and valuable discovery.

The English invaders are usually said to have come from three different barbarian tribes—Angles, Saxons and Jutes. The Angles and Saxons probably came from the borderlands of present-day Denmark and West Germany. But historians are still not sure about

The Nydam ship. It is similar to the Sutton Hoo ship, but a few feet shorter and more simply built

the Jutes. For centuries it was thought that their homeland was in the part of Denmark we call Jutland (Jute-land). Archaeologists now disagree with this. They have found remains in the lands round the mouth of the River Rhine similar to those in the Jutish parts of England.

One thing we are sure about is a link between the language of the English settlers and that spoken by the Frisians, who lived in the area which is now the Netherlands. This may mean that there had been some mixing of the tribes in Frisia before the invasions began. No doubt Frisians took part in the great movement of peoples, just as Angles, Saxons and Jutes did. The Frisians had a good reason for wanting to leave home. Their lands, mostly at or below sea-level, were often flooded, and they had to build homes on artificial mounds to raise them above the surrounding marshland.

The story of Hengest and Horsa

There are no written eyewitness accounts dating from the start of the English invasions, so we have to rely upon stories passed on and written down many years later by monks. Most of our information comes from the Venerable Bede, a monk who wrote a detailed history 300 years after the Romans left Britain (see Chap. 3).

It was the Angles that later gave their name to England (Angle-land). However, there is no evidence that they took a lead in the invasions. According to stories that have come down to us the first invaders to settle were a band of Jutes led by two brothers named Hengest and Horsa. We are told they came in three longboats, about the year 449.

The story goes that a local British king called Vortigern had invited Hengest and Horsa to come and help him fight the northern Picts. In return the Jutes were given the Isle of Thanet (which was not joined to the mainland, as it is today). But after sending for reinforcements from their homeland, the brothers turned against Vortigern. Horsa was killed, but Hengest overthrew the British leader and set up a kingdom of his own in Kent.

From then on a steady stream of settlers rowed across the sea to Britain. They sailed along the coasts and up the river estuaries— especially the Thames, Wash and Humber. The English invaders were primitive people who lived by hunting and farming. They were also very warlike. Beaching their longboats, they marched inland, killing plundering and burning as they went, taking all the best land from the Britons (whom they called *Welsh*—their word for foreigners).

The boats which carried these settlers were rowing galleys. They held about sixty to eighty people, thirty of them at the oars. We know this from various remains that have been found. The best example was discovered more than 100 years ago, preserved in a peat bog at Nydam, near the Danish-German border. The 'Nydam ship', built of oak planks, dates from about 400. Such ships must have been very unsafe because the sides were only just above the water-line. Shipwrecks would have been common in storms and rough seas.

Experts say that an open voyage straight across the North Sea would have been madness in a ship like this; especially as there

Nineteenth century artist's impression of King Arthur. He is shown here admitting Sir Tristram to the fellowship of the legendary Round Table

were no navigation charts or compasses. So the invaders almost certainly 'hugged the coastline' for most of the way. Perhaps they aimed to get to Cap Gris Nez, where Channel swimmers start or finish? From here the English coast is just over twenty miles away and can be seen on a clear day. Allowing for delays due to bad weather and the tiredness of the oarsmen, the longest passages must have taken two months or more.

A British revival—the legend of Arthur

Many Britons fled to escape the invaders. They went westwards, into the hills of what are now Cornwall and Devon, Wales, the Lake District and south-west Scotland. Some even crossed the seas, to Ireland or to Brittany in France. It must have been heartbreaking for them to leave their homes and crops, but even this was better than death or slavery.

However, in some areas the Britons gathered together and armed themselves. Where this happened the invaders met strong resistance. After perhaps half a century of gradual English settlement there seems to have been a British recovery. About the year 500 we are told that the Britons won a big battle at a place called Mount Badon. The invaders were driven out of a large part of the south Midlands, and their advance seems to have been checked for more than half a century.

According to legend several British victories at this time, including the one at Mount Badon, were inspired by a leader called King Arthur. It is likely that Arthur did in fact exist, but he would not have been much like the king in the famous stories of the Round Table. He would have been a war-chief, admired for his exploits in battle. His followers would not have been splendid knights like Sir Lancelot and Sir Galahad, although they may have fought on horseback. They would have been a band of brave Britons, fighting desperately to save their country from invasion.

The early English kingdoms

British resistance was courageous and skilful. But in the end it failed. By the middle of the sixth century the English were again advancing inland. In 577 they won a battle near Bath and reached the River Severn—thus cutting off the Britons in Wales from those in Devon and Cornwall.

By about 600 the Anglo-Saxons controlled most of what is now England, and also parts of southern Scotland. They had no liking for town life, so the cities of Roman Britain were left deserted. Houses, baths, temples and other fine buildings all crumbled into ruins. Weeds covered the Roman roads, which were now seldom used. Even the Roman villas in the countryside were left empty. The English settlers preferred to build their own rough timber huts, clustered together in villages surrounded by farm lands. This was the way of life they were used to.

Powerful chieftains who had led the invaders in battle now became local kings. In time the stronger kings conquered their weaker neighbours, so the number of separate kingdoms grew less.

By the year 600 there were roughly a dozen of them. But during the next 100 years or so three kingdoms emerged as the most powerful: Northumbria, Mercia and Wessex. Each grew strong fighting the Britons on its borders.

At first Northumbria (which simply means 'north of the Humber') was the biggest. It grew out of the two smaller kingdoms of Bernicia and Deira. These were united by Ethelfrith, a strong king of Bernicia, who ruled from about 593 to 616. At the end of his reign he won a great battle against the Britons near Chester. The northern English now controlled part of the west coast—thereby cutting off the Britons in Wales from those further north.

It took many centuries for all the British strongholds in the western hills to be conquered. But over the rest of the country—England—few traces of the Britons or their customs were left. The English we speak shows how complete the conquest was, because it contains only a handful of *Celtic* (British) words. Most of these are the names of natural features in the countryside; for example the Chiltern and Mendip Hills, and the rivers Esk, Exe, Usk and Ouse. Names of towns and villages are mostly Anglo-Saxon, having endings such as -ing, -ton, -ham, -hay, -stead, -ley, -ly or -leigh, -field, -ford, -pool, -water and -mouth.

Timescale

A.D.

400 Romans leave Britain

450 Hengest and Horsa   ENGLISH INVASIONS
                                       ↓

500 Battle of Mount Badon   BRITISH REVIVAL

550

     English reach the River Severn
600   ENGLISH
     Ethelfrith defeats Britons at Chester   TRIUMPHANT
                                       ↓

650 Sutton Hoo burial

More about the English invasions

Books

The Sutton Hoo Ship Burial (British Museum guide). For reference.

R. Sutcliff, *A Saxon Settler* (O.U.P., People of the Past).

A. F. Titterton, *Ships and Sailing* (Ginn's History Bookshelves, Blue Shelf). Pages 10–21.

B. Saklatvala, *Arthur, Roman Britain's Last Champion* (David and Charles Books).

B. K. Cooke, *King Arthur of Britain* (Edmund Ward).

Filmstrips

Sutton Hoo (*Daily Mail*, distributed by Educational Foundation for Visual Aids).

In Saxon Times (Visual Information Service).

Visit

The Sutton Hoo collection in the British Museum, London.

To write and find out

1 It is A.D. 500. Imagine your family has decided to sail to Britain from the land of the Saxons. Describe the voyage and landing. (Your story should be original, but based on an accurate historical background.)

2 Look at the map of the early English kingdoms. How many of these names of kingdoms are still used today in describing various parts of England? (You will need a good atlas.)

3 Many English place-names have the common Anglo-Saxon endings -*ton* (a farmstead or village), -*ham* (homestead, village) and -*ing* (place of a family or tribe.)
   (a) List the *ten* towns or villages nearest your home which have one of these endings.
   (b) On a blank outline map of England make a dot-map showing the overall distribution of *any one* of these place-name endings. (Start with the largest towns.)

2 The Roman Church — St Benedict and Gregory 'The Great'

St Benedict

About the year 500 a young man named Benedict left his comfortable home in central Italy and travelled to Rome. His parents, who were wealthy Christians, had sent him to finish his education and prepare to work in government service.

The Rome that greeted Benedict was very different from the proud city that for centuries ruled the Mediterranean world. During the previous 100 years it had suffered great destruction at the hands of 'barbarian' invaders from the north. They had ransacked public buildings, carrying away tons of valuables; melted down beautiful bronze statues, smashed stone monuments and left the streets littered with rubble. Even the great *aqueducts* (canals on bridges) which fed the city's taps and fountains were broken down or choked with vegetation.

The population had declined, and there were many open spaces where houses once stood. The palace of the emperors was deserted. The most important citizen was now the Bishop of Rome—the *Pope* (father) of the Church. There were still many Christians in western

Right: St Simeon Stylites, as shown in a modern film of his life
Below: Artist's impression of Rome being sacked by 'barbarians'

Europe, including barbarians who had been converted. Some of them at least still looked to Rome for leadership and guidance.

Italy was now ruled by Theodoric, leader of the barbarian East-Goths. From his capital at Ravenna, 200 miles from Rome, he did his best to bring back peace and order, encouraging Goths and Romans to be friends. But however hard he tried Theodoric could never restore the splendour of Rome and revive the spirit of its people.

St Benedict

Benedict was a deeply religious young man. He was shocked by the lawless and sinful behaviour of many Romans. So he gave up his studies, left the city and travelled eastwards to the hills. There, on the mountain of Subiaco, he found a cave and became a hermit. To Benedict it seemed the best way of getting closer to God and living a truly Christian life.

This was not a new idea. Christ himself had told a rich young man: 'If you would be perfect, go, sell what you possess and give to the poor, and you will have treasure in Heaven; and come, follow me.' Long before Benedict was born, men in Egypt and other eastern Mediterranean lands had gone into the deserts to escape the wickedness of the world and be alone with their God. Such men were called *monks*. The word really means 'one who lives alone', but often monks gathered in communities, working and praying together. This way of life soon spread to parts of the West, including Ireland.

The earliest monks believed it did them good to suffer unnecessary hardships. They cut out 'luxuries' like soft beds and comfortable clothes. They fasted for long periods and spent night after night praying instead of sleeping. Some went to extremes, whipping themselves, rolling naked among thorns or trying to set up new records of endurance and self-sacrifice. In the Syrian desert, St Simeon Stylites worshipped God from a platform on top of a tall pillar. There was no room to lie down and no protection from the blazing sun. To get food and drink Simeon lowered a basket on the end of a rope. Yet he stayed up there for thirty-three years! St Daniel, one of his followers, later beat his 'record' by three months.

Such record-breaking achievements did not interest Benedict. Once when he saw a hermit chained to a rock he said: 'If you are God's servant, let the chain of Christ not any iron chain hold thee.' Although he wore skins and ate dry bread, Benedict attempted, as he put it, 'nothing harsh nor burdensome'. Before long, religious men in Rome heard about the monk in the hills and went to visit him. Some asked if they could stay and share his quiet, simple life. So Benedict organised a community of monks who all agreed to give up worldly pleasures and pray to God.

After some years Benedict left Subiaco with a small band of his closest followers. They travelled south, to the top of a hill overlooking the village of Monte Cassino, and there, about the year 525, Benedict founded his most famous monastery. He lived at Monte Cassino until his death in 543. Some of the time he spent writing a *Rule* for monks to live by. This 'Benedictine Rule', which is in fact a large number of rules, is still practised today in many countries.

The Benedictine 'Rule'

St Benedict's idea of a monastery was a place where ordinary men would want to come and lead a Christian life, praying and working together. He ordered that the monks' clothes, although plain, should be warm and comfortable. They were to have a good eight hours of sleep, and two daily meals of simple but nourishing food.

Nevertheless it was still not an easy life in a Benedictine monastery. The abbot, elected by the brothers to rule the community, had to be obeyed at all times, without the slightest question or delay. Through regular obedience a monk would always be humble and never get a high opinion of himself. As Benedict put it: 'Everywhere, sitting or walking or standing, let him always be with his . . . looks fixed upon the ground; remembering every hour that he is guilty of his sins.'

No personal belongings were allowed. Even a monk's clothes were the property of the monastery. 'No one, without the abbot's permission,' wrote Benedict, 'shall presume to give, receive or keep for himself, anything whatsoever; neither book, nor writing tablets nor pen.' A monk could not even receive a letter from his parents without the abbot's agreement. On top of this there were strict rules about silence. The monks were rarely allowed to speak to each other. And it goes without saying that all relationships with women were forbidden.

Only a truly devoted Christian would be able to keep such difficult rules. So Benedict ordered that each newcomer, or *novice,* would have a year 'on probation' before having to make his solemn promises of obedience to the Rule. But once he had promised he was

Monte Cassino today

Part of the interior of Monte Cassino

Position of Benedict's monasteries

Right: Modern Benedictine monks doing their own building. All work is done for God and is considered to be a form of prayer

expected to belong to the monastery all his life. He could not step outside the walls without the abbot's permission. 'He must know', wrote Benedict, 'that he has henceforth no power even over his own body.'

The daily life of the community began before dawn, and every part of it was timetabled. At regular intervals all the brothers gathered in their chapel to pray and sing God's praises. There were eight separate services each day, which took about five hours altogether. The rest of the time was fully occupied, for, as Benedict said: 'Idleness is the enemy of the soul. And therefore, at fixed times, the brothers ought to be occupied in manual labour; and at other fixed hours, in holy reading.' So every day except Sunday about seven hours were spent doing ordinary work such as farming, cooking, cleaning, caring for the sick, writing and copying books, or teaching boys and younger monks.

St Benedict's *Rule* was practical and full of common sense. In the years to come monasteries all over Europe copied it. Nuns too lived according to its basic vows of *obedience, poverty* (no belongings) and *chastity* (no sexual relationships). Later, some 'double houses' were founded, where both monks and nuns lived under the rule of an abbess. The sexes were carefully kept apart. At one double house in England the abbess would only speak to the monks through a window!

In those troubled times Benedictine monasteries were almost the only places where people could find peace, order and good living. The example they set encouraged ordinary Christians to live better lives. Monasteries were also centres of learning and education. Monks taught the young, kept historical records and made copies of the Scriptures and many other books. Without their efforts most of the writings of the ancient world would have been unknown in the barbarian kingdoms of the West.

Gregory 'the Great'

In Benedict's lifetime the *Rule* was only followed in monasteries he set up himself. It later became famous mainly through the efforts of a pope—Gregory I, called 'the Great'.

Like Benedict, Gregory was born into a wealthy family, about the year 540. His father had a large house in Rome and could afford to give his son a good education. Gregory soon showed outstanding ability. He was only in his early thirties when he was chosen *Prefect* of Rome, the highest position in the government of the city.

It was a time of great hardship for the people. Italy was again being invaded by barbarians—the fierce Lombards ('Longbeards') who came from north Germany. Pouring through the passes in the Alps, they quickly overran most of northern Italy (part of this area is still called Lombardy today). Seeing all the misery and destruction around him, Gregory felt sure the world was coming to an end. 'Beaten down by so many blows', he wrote, 'the ancient kingdom [Rome] has fallen from its glory and shows us now another kingdom [Heaven], which is coming, which is already near.'

After only a year as *Prefect,* Gregory decided to give up his position and devote his life to serving God. His father had just died, leaving a large fortune. Gregory gave some to charity and used the rest to set up six monasteries in Sicily. His own house in Rome was turned into a seventh, and there Gregory became a monk. As a writer of the time put it: 'He who had before gone about the city . . . in silk and jewels, [was] now clothed in a humble garment.'

Pope Gregory gives his blessing to a man possessed by the devil

Not long afterwards some monks from Monte Cassino arrived in Rome. They had gone there to escape the attacks of the Lombards. We cannot be certain, but it was probably from these monks that Gregory first learned about the *Rule* of St Benedict. It was a great inspiration to him and he put it into practice in his own monastery. Later he wrote about Benedict's life and work, making it known to Christians in many countries.

'The first of the great popes'

The most important part of Gregory's life began in 590, a year of floods and plague, when he was chosen to be Pope. By then his health was failing. Yet right up to his death in 604, he worked tirelessly to strengthen the organisation of the Church and unite Christians in many lands. He kept in close contact with bishops and clergy, and wrote a special handbook called *The Pastoral Rule,* which instructed them how to carry out their duties.

Above all Gregory worked to spread the faith among heathens. The barbarian king of Spain was converted by missionaries sent by Gregory, and most of the King's subjects soon became Christians. Gregory also sent a band of monks to convert the English. The outcome of this important mission is described in the next chapter.

The throne of Gregory the Great

The Church was only part of Gregory's concern. He considered himself directly responsible for all the poor and plague-stricken people of Rome. Whenever he heard that a beggar had died of hunger in the streets he blamed himself for it. As Pope, Gregory received the income from a number of large estates. He used most of it to provide free food, clothing and medical care for the needy. He even organised the defence of Rome against the Lombards, and finally made a peace treaty with them.

Nothing seemed too difficult for Gregory, or too small to escape his attention. The vast amount of work he got through can be seen from the hundreds of letters he wrote, which are still preserved. They were addressed not only to Church leaders and missionaries, but also to kings, queens and tribal chiefs. In a time of invasions, plagues and famines, the organisation of the Roman Church might easily have collapsed, just like the Roman Empire, had it not been for Gregory's work. He has been rightly called 'the first of the great popes'.

More about Benedict and Gregory

The story of medieval monasteries is continued in Chapter 15.

Books

Most books on medieval monasteries (some are listed at the end of Chapter 15) begin with a section on St Benedict. For example:

M. E. Reeves, *The Medieval Monastery* (Longman, Then and There series). Chapter 2.

F. A. Gasquet (Ed.), *The Rule of St Benedict* (Chatto and Windus, Medieval Library series). For reference.

Venerable Bede, *A History of the English Church and People* (Penguin Classics.) Book 2, Chapter 1 refers to Pope Gregory.

Gregory the Great (hands upraised) leads a procession to pray for the end of a dreadful plague in Rome (590)

Visit

The ruins of a Benedictine monastery in England. Examples include Glastonbury (Somerset), Jarrow (Durham), St Albans (Herts) and Abingdon (Berks). Make a plan of the site.

To write and find out

1 *(a)* Draw up a list of instructions you imagine Gregory may have given the missionaries he sent to convert the heathens in Spain and England. What dangers and difficulties might he have warned them of?

   (b) Why do you think Gregory was called 'the Great'?

2 Why did monks think it so important to lead a life of hardship? In what ways was St Benedict's *Rule* 'full of common sense'?

3 In the Second World War there was a great battle at Monte Cassino. Find out who fought in the battle and what happened to the monastery.

3 Heathens Become Christians

Christianity first came to Britain when the country was part of the Roman Empire. But the English invaders were heathens, so Christian worship died out wherever they settled. The English wore charms to keep away evil spirits, and they believed giants, dragons and other monsters lived in the lonely moors, woods and swamps. They worshipped nature gods, making sacrifices to them at certain seasons. In the autumn, when many cattle were slaughtered, there were great ceremonial feastings.

Chief among their gods was *Woden.* Nearly all Anglo-Saxon kings claimed they were descended from him. Other gods included *Tiw,* a war-god; *Thunor,* god of thunder, which was believed to be the sound of his chariot rolling across the heavens; and *Frig,* a goddess who was supposed to bring good harvests. All of these are still remembered in our days of the week—Tuesday (Tiw), Wednesday (Woden), Thursday (Thunor) and Friday (Frig). Saturday probably comes from *Saturn,* the Roman god of agriculture. Sunday and Monday are named after the sun and moon, both worshipped by the Anglo-Saxons.

The heathen English certainly expected some kind of future life. Otherwise they would not have buried the goods of the dead—as at Sutton Hoo. But we cannot be sure what kind of after-world they believed in.

Bronze plate of an Anglo-Saxon god

St Augustine

Augustine's mission

We are told that some years before he became Pope, Gregory the Great was struck by the sight of some fair-haired, light-skinned boys being sold as slaves in a Roman market place. He learned that they were Angles from Northumbria. It shocked him to think that such fine young men were ignorant of the Word of God.

When he became Pope, Gregory decided to send missionaries to convert the English. He assembled a party of about forty monks from his own monastery in Rome. Under their leader, Augustine, they landed on the Isle of Thanet, in Kent, early in 597. The king of Kent, Ethelbert, already had a Christian wife called Bertha. She was a princess from the kingdom of the Franks (now France) which had been converted a hundred years before. Ethelbert himself was still a pagan. But he agreed to meet Augustine, as long as it was in the open air, where he believed his visitors would be unable to work their 'magic' on him!

Ethelbert must have been surprised by the sight of shaven-headed monks, wearing black Benedictine robes and chanting in a strange language. But he decided to trust them. He gave them food and shelter in Canterbury and allowed them to preach to his people. With Queen Bertha's permission, the monks used the old Roman church of St Martin—one of the few not destroyed in the invasions.

Before the year was out Ethelbert had been baptised a Christian, and so had thousands of his people. Soon more converts were gained in the neighbouring kingdoms of Essex and East Anglia. It was an encouraging start. Gregory made Augustine Archbishop of Canterbury and sent him instructions on how to organise the English Church. He advised Augustine not to destroy the pagan temples but to change them into churches, replacing the idols with altars. Gregory also suggested that the old heathen sacrifices could be turned into the regular Christian festivals. Thus Christmas replaced the winter feast of Yule, and Easter is still named after a Saxon spring goddess, *Eostre*.

The Roman mission finally took root in England, but not before it had suffered a series of setbacks. Gregory died in 604 and Augustine at about the same time. Soon afterwards there was a return to paganism in many parts of south-eastern England. In East Anglia, King Redwald decided to have the best of both worlds. He kept two altars in the same temple; one for Christ and one for the heathen gods!

The only bright spot was the conversion of Edwin, king of Northumbria. He married a Christian daughter of Ethelbert in 625, and within two years her chaplain had baptised the King and many of his subjects. But then disaster struck the kingdom. In 632 Edwin was defeated and killed by the pagan king of Mercia. The Queen fled to Kent with her children, while many of the people returned to their old heathen ways. The northern English were soon brought back to Christianity, but not by the Roman missionaries.

The Church of St Martin at Canterbury, used by Augustine's mission. It still has a few Roman bricks in its walls today

On the right-hand side of this whalebone casket, made in Northumbria in the seventh century, we see the Three Wise Kings bearing their gifts. The flower-like object above is the guiding star

Christians from Ireland

Right through the years of Anglo-Saxon settlement the Christian faith had been kept alive in the unconquered western parts of Britain. Ireland in particular became a stronghold of Christianity through the efforts of St Patrick, a Briton who became a monk in Gaul. In the middle of the fifth century Patrick travelled throughout Ireland preaching and baptising the people. After about thirty years he and his followers had made Ireland a Christian country.

A century later, in 563, an Irish monk named Columba sailed across to the land of the heathen Picts. On the tiny island of Iona he and twelve other monks set up a monastery. First they cleared the land and planted crops. Then they began to convert the Picts in the Highlands. When Columba died (in 597 – the year Augustine landed in Kent) the English were the only people in the British Isles who had not heard the teachings of Christ.

Iona remained an important centre of the British, or *Celtic*, Church. It was from there that Christianity came back to northern England after the death of King Edwin in 632. The next Northumbrian king, Oswald, had been Edwin's rival. He spent many years in exile on Iona, where he learnt the Christian teachings from Columba's followers. Naturally when he became king he turned to Iona for help in restoring the faith among his people. A small company of Irish monks arrived in 635, under their leader Aidan. They chose to build their monastery on the island of Lindisfarne. This is just off the coast, although at low tide it is possible to walk across the sands to the mainland.

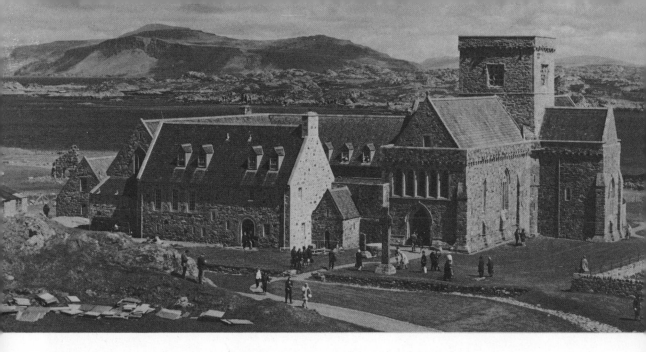

Aidan and his companions travelled on foot all over the hills and dales of northern England, preaching, setting up monasteries and training monks. Some of them later travelled south to preach to the peoples of Mercia, East Anglia and Essex. Although King Oswald was killed in battle (642) the work of Aidan and his monks went on, encouraged by the new king, Oswy. Lindisfarne was so famous as a place of God that it was called 'Holy Island'.

The synod at Whitby
Christianity thus came to the English by two quite separate routes. Roman missionaries converted many people in the South, bringing them into the Roman *Catholic* (or universal) Church. But the conversion of the North and Midlands was led by 'Celtic' Christians from Iona.

For more than 200 years these Celts had been cut off from the rest of the Christian world. Consequently they had developed many of their own customs and practices. They had a different baptism service; celebrated Easter at an earlier date than other Christians, and did not follow the leadership of the Pope. Celtic monks even had a different *tonsure* (haircut). Instead of shaving the crown of the head, which was usual, they shaved a semicircular patch in front, from ear to ear.

All these differences caused much confusion. In the Northumbrian court King Oswy followed Celtic practices, while his queen (Edwin's daughter who escaped to Kent) had been taught the Roman ways. So Easter was celebrated twice in the same household.

Oswy wanted to bring all English Christians together. In 663 he called a *synod*, or council, of the Northumbrian Church at Whitby. Christian leaders from all over the country were invited. The main business of the meeting was to agree on the dating of Easter. But

The different tonsures of Celtic and Roman monks

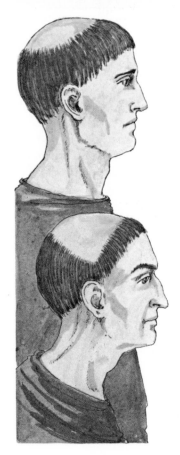

behind this lay a much bigger question. Were the Celtic Christians willing to accept the leadership of the Roman Church?

Speaking for the Roman side was Wilfred, abbot of a monastery at Ripon, who had spent some years on the Continent. 'Our Easter customs,' he said, 'are generally observed . . . in all the world wherever the Church of Christ has spread. The only people . . . to disagree with the whole world are these Scots and their obstinate supporters, the Picts and Britons.' In the end Wilfred's arguments convinced Oswy, and the Roman Church won the day. All present agreed with the King, except a few Celtic monks who went back to Iona.

From now on English bishops were in touch with Rome and other parts of Europe. Gradually, during the next century, Celtic Christians in Scotland, Ireland and Wales came to accept Roman customs.

Theodore and Boniface

Soon after the meeting at Whitby the Pope had to appoint a new Archbishop of Canterbury. He chose a wise and scholarly Greek monk named Theodore, who was then living in Rome. Theodore arrived in England in 669 and continued the task of uniting both Celtic and Roman Christians in one Church. The decision taken at Whitby was only a first step. Theodore held regular councils of bishops from both sides to help sort out the many differences that remained.

The Celtic Church was based on monasteries. But the Roman Church was organised differently. Countries were divided into large districts called *dioceses,* each under a bishop with a cathedral church. Dioceses were sub-divided into *parishes,* each with a priest to serve the religious needs of the people. Theodore increased the number of dioceses and appointed many new bishops. He also saw that schools were set up for training the much needed parish priests. But this was a very long task. Even 300 years later there were still some villages which had no regular priest and no church.

Church building was costly. Most people had to do without a parish church until perhaps a wealthy lord built one. In the mean-

The abbey of Iona today, with the island of Mull in the background

Escomb Church in County Durham. Built in the seventh or eighth century, it is still almost complete today

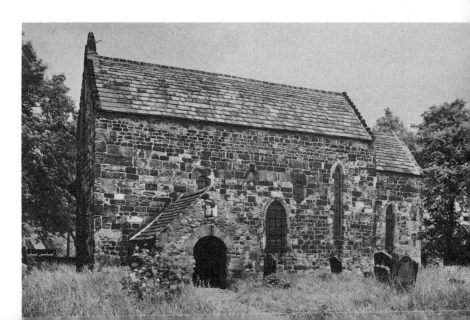

time monks or priests set up large crosses in the open air, and villagers gathered round them for services. Theodore gave priests special permission to hold the service of mass 'in the field'. Some of these 'wayside crosses' were made of rough wood. Others were built of stone and delicately carved.

One of the finest stone crosses can still be seen at Ruthwell, near Dumfries, where it is now inside the village church. It is eighteen feet high and has beautiful carvings on it, some showing scenes from the life of Jesus. Down the sides there is part of an Old English poem, *The Dream of the Rood.* The Rood is the cross of Christ, and it tells how it felt when the Son of God hung upon it: 'I trembled in his clasp, yet dared not bow nor fall to earth. . . They pierced me with dark nails, you see the wounds . . . stained was I with the blood that streamed.'

Even before the last pagans had been converted at home, English monks began preaching on the Continent—in the homelands of their ancestors. In 690, the year of Theodore's death, a Northumbrian monk named Willibrord sailed to Frisia with a dozen companions. For almost fifty years he worked to convert the people, and founded several monasteries and churches. The Pope made Willibrord bishop over the part of Frisia he had brought into the Church.

The greatest of all Anglo-Saxon missionaries was Boniface, a monk from Wessex. In 718 he left England, never to return. Travelling deep into the heart of heathen Germany, he personally converted thousands of people in the lands east of the Rhine. His progress was closely followed in Rome, and also back in England. He often wrote to English friends for help and advice. Boniface eventually became an archbishop and set about organising the first Christian Church in Germany. Englishmen who went out to help him became abbots of new monasteries, priests and even bishops.

Boniface was never at rest. When he was well over seventy he left Germany to work among the Frisians (many were still pagans). But there the 'Apostle of Germany' met his death. Just after dawn on 5 June 754, Boniface was about to confirm some new converts when a band of pagans appeared and brutally murdered him, together with many of his companions.

Bede—scholar of Northumbria

Most of our knowledge of the English conversions comes from the *History of the English Church and People,* completed in 731 by the monk Bede. In fact, without this book the previous 300 years of English history would be almost a blank page! Bede grew up in Northumbria at the time of Archbishop Theodore. It was an unusual childhood, because when he was seven his parents entrusted him to the care of monks at Wearmouth—a fine new Benedictine monastery.

The abbot, Benedict Biscop, spent many years studying and travelling in Italy and France. He brought stonemasons and other craftsmen from the Continent to build Wearmouth—and also a second monastery he founded nearby at Jarrow. But more important for the future of Bede, Biscop returned from several visits to Rome with large quantities of books. His monasteries soon had libraries as good as any in England.

The Ruthwell Cross

The conversion of the English, from north and south

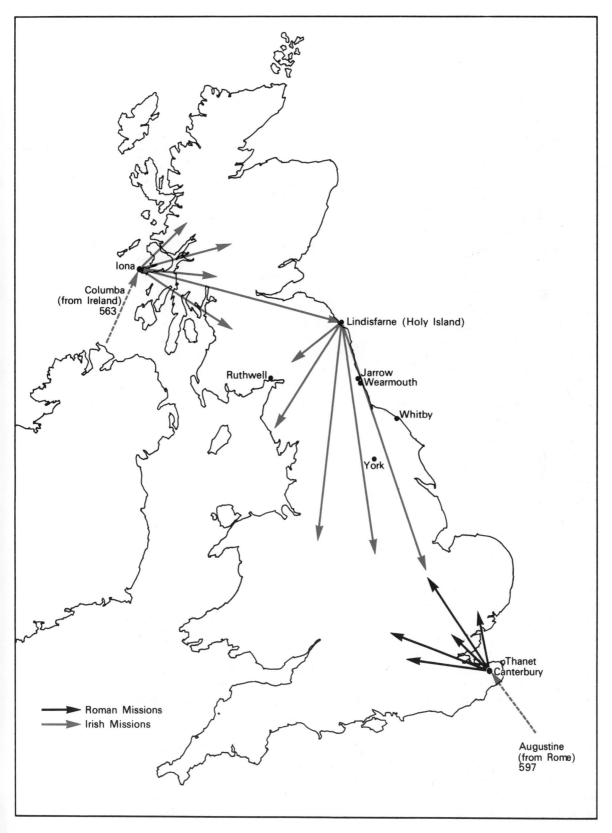

Iona

Columba
(from Ireland)
563

Lindisfarne (Holy Island)

Ruthwell

Jarrow
Wearmouth

Whitby

York

Thanet
Canterbury

Augustine
(from Rome)
597

→ Roman Missions
→ Irish Missions

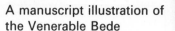

Bede left Wearmouth when he was still a boy and spent the rest of his life at Jarrow. It took him many years to collect all the information for his *History*. He carefully studied old Anglo-Saxon stories, songs and poems. Monks from all over the country sent documents, and some came to talk to him. A priest from London even visited Rome for Bede, to look at Pope Gregory's letters to Augustine. The finished work, written in Latin, was very detailed yet clear and easy to read.

Bede's *History* was almost the last of a long series of books, which earned him the name 'Venerable' (worthy of respect). He is sometimes called 'the father of English learning'. Most of his writings were explanations of the Scriptures, or textbooks for pupils in the monastery school. Bede considered himself to be mainly a teacher. At a time when there were no ordinary schools, education was chiefly carried on in monasteries. Nearly all books were in Latin, the language of the Scriptures and church services.

In 735, the year of Bede's death, York became the home of a second archbishop. From then on York cathedral school was the main centre of learning in Northumbria. Its library was one of the best in western Europe. Alcuin, master of the school for fifteen years, later went to the court of Charlemagne, king of the Franks. He did much to spread Northumbrian standards of education on the Continent.

There were educated people in all parts of England—not just Northumbria—as we know from the southerners who helped Bede or wrote to Boniface in Germany. Archbishop Theodore set up an excellent cathedral school at Canterbury which taught Greek as well as Latin. Thus the Christian conversions helped to civilise the once barbarous English. By the time of Bede and Alcuin they had become famous for their faith and learning.

Right: Irish missionaries taught Northumbrian monks the art of beautiful writing, and book decoration with coloured inks. This is a decorated page from a famous copy of the four Gospels made at Lindisfarne, about AD 700. The 'Lindisfarne Gospels' which are kept in the British Museum, have gold, silver and jewels set in the cover

More about the English conversions

Books

F. Grice, *A Northumbrian Missionary* (O.U.P., People of the Past).

R. W. Thomson, *How Christianity Came to England* (Religious Education Press).

Venerable Bede, *A History of the English Church and People* (Penguin Classics). For reference.

Filmstrip

The Conversion of the English, 3 Parts (Society for the Promotion of Christian Knowledge).

Visits

Crosses at Ruthwell (6 miles west of Annan, Dumfriesshire) and Bewcastle (20 miles north-east of Carlisle).

Saxon churches: Escomb (Durham), Hexham (Northumberland), Wing (Bucks), Corhampton (Hants) or Bradford-on-Avon (Wilts).

To write and find out

1 Write down some of the arguments you think would have been put by each side at the Synod of Whitby. Perhaps put it in the form of a dialogue between Wilfred and Colman, Bishop of Lindisfarne, who was the main spokesman for the Celtic side.

2 How would Augustine's journey from Rome to England compare with a journey over the same route today?

3 *(a)* St Cuthbert was a famous prior of Lindisfarne and bishop of Northumbria a few years after Aidan. Find out about his life. What happened to his coffin after his death?

   (b) Irish people are very proud of St Patrick, their patron saint. Find out more about him. Talk to some Irishmen if you can.

Part of the manuscript of
Beowulf

4 Early English Life and Customs

It is difficult to find out about the lives of ordinary people in the early English kingdoms. Monks who kept historical records usually wrote only about kings and churchmen. Even then, most of the kings are just names to us. We usually know the dates of their reigns and the battles they fought. But we have no pictures of them and little idea of what they were like as people.

All we have left are some of their possessions—armour, weapons, jewels, rings and perhaps coins. Their wooden buildings and furniture have rotted away, so to imagine the halls kings lived in we must turn to the works of poets. Old English was mainly a spoken language. Only a tiny fraction of Anglo-Saxon verse was written down and preserved. But luckily we have all 3,182 lines of *Beowulf,* a stirring tale of kings and warriors, composed in England by a Christian poet, probably some time in the eighth century.

'The joys of the hall'

A drinking horn and tumblers of the kind used in Anglo-Saxon banquets, where they were filled with ale or mead

Beowulf, the hero of the poem, goes to help the Danish king and his followers, who are living in fear of an evil monster called Grendel. After a fierce struggle Beowulf overcomes the monster, and then dives into the sea to kill its mother in her under-water cave. Years later he becomes a king himself, and has to rescue his people from a terrible dragon which destroys their homes with its fiery breath. The aged Beowulf slays the dragon in its lair; but in the struggle he is wounded and dies.

The story is a fairy tale, yet its background helps us to understand the way real kings and their followers lived. For instance the Danish king, Hrothgar, had a banqueting hall which was a large barn-like building made of wood. To celebrate Beowulf's killing of Grendel, we are told that Hrothgar decorated its walls with golden tapestries and had a great feast prepared. The guests drank toasts of mead, an intoxicating drink made with honey, and then, 'Hrothgar gave Beowulf an embroidered banner of gold, a helmet and a mail-coat . . . He also ordered eight horses with golden bridles to be led . . . inside the hall.'

The helmet presented to Beowulf had 'round the top . . . a projecting rim', which gave the wearer extra protection against a sword blow. It is interesting to compare the poet's description with the helmet found at Sutton Hoo (turn back to the picture in Chapter 1). A strengthening rim of iron can be seen running over the top.

When Beowulf had been honoured the feasting and drinking proceeded. Entertainments were provided by minstrels and poets: 'Songs were sung in Hrothgar's presence to the accompaniment of music. The harp was struck, and many ballads recited' . . . laughter rang out, cup-bearers poured wine from wonderfully made flagons.'

The evening closed with a visit from the queen, who carried a jewelled goblet round the hall for all to drink. The royal couple left to sleep in a separate chamber, but the king's followers, or *thanes*, stayed in the hall. 'Benches were cleared away and pillows and bedding spread upon the floor.' The warriors slept with their weapons close at hand, for '. . . it was their practice to be ready to fight at any moment'.

This reminds us that there was more to a thane's life than 'the joys of the hall'. He had to serve and protect his lord at all times. Thanes accompanied the king when he rode out to hunt the stag, fox and wild boar. They also went on longer expeditions, to fight wars and help keep law and order in the kingdom. A king's power depended on the loyalty, strength and courage of his thanes.

Kings and thanes

In Bede's *History*, the Christian kings of Northumbria seem peace-loving, almost saintly men. Priests and monks were honoured members of their household. No doubt this was true, but it is a rather one-sided picture. Bede was not a fighting man. From *Beowulf* we get a more down-to-earth view of kings surrounded by their warriors.

In the poem we see how important it was for a king to have plenty of gold and precious things. He had to be able to give costly gifts to his queen and followers, and clothe himself in fine robes and armour suitable for a ruler. No expense was spared to satisfy these needs. Remember the Sutton Hoo ship contained weapons and treasures from as far away as the Mediterranean lands.

Whether they were God-fearing men or not, successful kings had to be brave and generous. Thanes, above all, had to be loyal to their lord and die for him if necessary. King Edwin of Northumbria was once attacked by an assassin with a dagger. Lilla, one of his thanes, quickly thrust his own body in the way of the attacker and himself took the deadly blows aimed at the King.

In return for their services thanes expected to be given weapons, horses and other gifts; and also food and drink—'the joys of the hall'. The most valuable gift of all was land, the real basis of wealth and power. Once he had an estate, a thane could marry and set up his own household. But he still served the king faithfully, even though no longer a member of his bodyguard.

From time to time each king called together an assembly of thanes, to discuss new laws, gifts of land and other such matters. Church leaders were also invited—bishops, abbots of the larger monasteries and perhaps the king's own priests. This assembly was called a *Witan*. The word means 'wise men', although not everyone who attended was necessarily wise.

In those days a king did not have a capital. He travelled around the royal estates, and the Witan met wherever he happened to be. Its members only offered advice when the king asked for it, and even then he would make up his own mind. But at least his decisions were more widely known if they were witnessed by a gathering of important subjects. As kingdoms got bigger meetings of the Witan became more important, and kings had to appoint special government officials.

No single king was strong enough to gain control of the whole

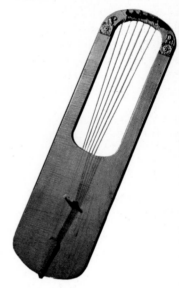

A six-stringed harp, pieced together from fragments found at Sutton Hoo. This must have been the kind of instrument mentioned in *Beowulf*

The dotted line marks the remains of part of Offa's dyke, pictured near Wrexham

country until the tenth century. But in the meantime some rulers came near to being kings of all England. In the seventh century the rule of the Northumbrian kings often reached down as far as the River Thames. In the eighth century Mercia became even stronger, under Ethelbald (716–57) and Offa (757–96). Both were overlords of most of England. They made lesser kings come to ask favours and fight under their leadership in war.

Offa built a great dyke (ditch and bank) to mark the frontier between Mercia and the Britons in Wales. Today, twelve centuries later, parts of Offa's dyke can still be seen, winding their way between the estuary of the River Dee and the Bristol Channel. When

The three great English kingdoms, seventh to ninth centuries

he died Offa was overlord of all England below the Humber. But after him the power of Mercia crumbled. King Egbert of Wessex defeated the Mercians in 825 and made himself master of the southern English. By Egbert's reign (802–39) there were only three or four separate kingdoms left in England. Soon Wessex would be the *only* one. The others were overrun by the Vikings, as we will see in Chapter 7.

Churls and thralls

The ordinary people in each kingdom farmed the land or worked in village trades. Most were free-men called *churls*; but there were also *thralls,* or slaves. From laws and other early documents we can get some idea of the way these 'lower orders' of society lived.

Many thralls were descended from the unfortunate Britons who lost their lands to the English invaders. In fact the word Briton was often used to mean 'a slave'. Other thralls were prisoners taken

Dress in Anglo-Saxon England

A THANE (king's follower, or nobleman) and his wife. Their clothes are finer in quality and more decorative than those of the churl and his wife. The thane's cloak is made of fur, his tunic of wool, his belt and shoes of softer leather. Notice his ornamental brooch, belt buckle and pouch. Anglo-Saxon men seem to have worn jewellery just as much as women. His wife wears over her petticoat and linen dress a light cloak called a mantle. The head was put through the middle, so the mantle hung down both back and front

A CHURL (peasant farmer) and his wife. The man's coarse linen tunic is like a knee-length shirt. His feet and legs are wrapped in linen and cross-gartered up to the knees. In winter a short cloak was worn, with a hood attached. His wife's tunic is full length, and it was usual for women to cover their heads. Both use brooches to fasten their cloaks and have shoes made of rough leather

31

The wergeld

in wars between the kingdoms, or criminals unable to pay the fines imposed on them. In very hard times, when people were dying of starvation, parents might sell their children into slavery if they had no food for them.

Children of thralls were themselves unfree. So slavery carried on, even though Church leaders disapproved of it. If a bishop had thralls on his estate he would probably free them in his will. Slaves were allowed to earn money for extra work. So some managed to save up and buy their freedom. But if a thrall ran away and was caught he was put to death.

Churls were mostly peasant farmers, owning a *hide*—a piece of land large enough to support an ordinary household. The size of a hide varied from place to place, but it was somewhere between fifty and a hundred acres. The churl and his family lived in a simple wooden hut; its roof thatched with straw, reeds or heather. Inside there was probably one all-purpose room. In cold weather a fire burned in an open hearth and the smoke escaped through a hole in the roof. Nearby there may have been outbuildings for storing grain and keeping tools.

A document written in later years stated that 'If a churl prospered, so that he had fully five hides of land . . . and special duties in the king's hall, then he was henceforward worthy of the rank of a thane.' But as time went by it became more difficult for churls to better themselves. Their holdings of land seem to have got smaller rather than larger, and the differences in wealth between the nobles and the rest increased.

The folk-moot

The chief mark distinguishing the ranks of thane, churl and thrall was the *wergeld.* This was a man's 'life-price'—the number of oxen

Reconstruction of a Saxon peasant's home, based on the findings of archaeologists near Bourton-on-the-Water in Gloucestershire. The hut measures 20 feet by 12½ feet. It has no windows, so light must have come in through an open doorway

An Anglo-Saxon king with his Witan, or assembly of thanes. It seems that a wrongdoer has been condemned to death; we can see him being hanged on the right of the picture

or the sum of money that had to be paid to his relatives by any man who killed him. Wergelds were fixed according to rank. In the early laws of Wessex, a nobleman's life-price was six times that of a churl. It was much the same elsewhere, except in Kent where churls had a greater value. Thralls had no wergeld.

Early English law was based on the wergeld, and on the duties of the *kindred* (relatives). Nowadays we try to keep law and order by having police, prisons and so on. But in those days it was fear of the kindred that helped to prevent crime. If a man was killed, injured or wronged in any way, his kindred would either take vengeance on the person responsible or claim compensation based on his wergeld.

Kings and church leaders encouraged the peaceful method of settlement, in money or goods. But if the wrongdoer would not, or could not, pay compensation, vengeance ('the blood feud') was the only alternative. Some crimes, such as treachery to one's lord, were so serious that compensation was not enough. The penalty was death, usually by hanging. Other kinds of punishment, such as imprisonment on the king's estate, were rarely mentioned in the laws. However, if an accused man failed to appear and answer a charge against him he was declared an *outlaw* and could be killed by anyone.

The people held regular open-air meetings, or *folk-moots,* to deal with law-breakers, among other things. In law courts today both

Trial by ordeal

sides try to produce evidence about the facts of the case. But Anglo-Saxon customs were different. The *defendant* (the person accused) was usually asked to swear a solemn oath that he was innocent. Then he had to bring forward 'oath-helpers', who would swear that his oath was true.

The value of an oath-helper depended on his rank. The word of a thane or bishop was worth much more than that of a churl. If enough of the right sort of oath-helpers were produced the case was over. Sometimes the right to swear an oath belonged to the other side—the *plaintiff*. This happened in cases where the defendant was caught in the act or was a suspicious character who had been accused before.

If not enough oath-helpers could be found the judgment usually depended upon *trial by ordeal*. A priest took charge and asked the defendant to choose either iron or water. In the ordeal of cold water he was thrown into a pond or river. It was believed that the water would cast out the guilty, who floated, yet 'receive' the innocent, who sank!

The ordeal by iron was a 'burn test'. The defendant carried a red hot iron bar for nine feet. Then his hand was bandaged, and if the wound healed in three days without festering he was declared innocent. Sometimes a burn test was done with boiling water. The defendant plunged his hand into it to take out a stone. The idea behind all these 'ordeals' was that God would give a judgment by helping only the innocent.

Farming and trading

The countryside in this period was mostly wild and uninhabited. There were great stretches of moor, marshland and dense forest where wolves, wild boar and herds of deer roamed. Many of the English settlers took over lands cleared by the Britons. But in some places they began to tame the wilderness and establish new village communities. They made forest clearings, used the timber for building and for fuel, and divided up the land for farming.

Each family had a share of the arable (plough) land of the village. Sometimes good and bad soil was evenly distributed by giving every family a number of separate plots scattered about two or three large fields. This is called 'open field' farming (see Chapter 11).

The chief crops were cereals—barley, rye and wheat—which were made into bread. Barley was also used in brewing beer. Peas, beans and flax were often grown, and bees were kept. Honey was essential, because in those days people had no sugar, so it was the only kind of sweetening. On the wasteland bordering the village families kept a few cattle, sheep or pigs.

Most villages had a 'lord'—one of the king's thanes—whom the people looked to for protection. The lord had a good share of the land and the villagers farmed it for him. Besides giving this free labour they paid regular 'food rent', in wheat, pigs, eggs and so on, which they carried up to the lord's hall.

Not all villagers farmed the land. Some carried on the necessary trades. Smiths made tools and implements, including ploughs,

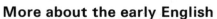

shovels, pots and pans; and there were also carpenters, shoemakers and others. Weavers and bakers were not so necessary, because most women spun and wove their own rough garments and baked bread on the hearth. Highly skilled craftsmen such as goldsmiths, stone-masons and weapon-makers were usually employed by kings.

Each village supplied most of its own essential needs. But a few things were brought in from outside by travelling pedlars. In carts or on horseback they carried wool, iron for smiths and salt for preserving the winter's store of meat. Travel was difficult along rough tracks or paths. It was also dangerous, and pedlars might band together for safety in case they were attacked by outlaws hiding in the woods.

There was a regular sea trade across the Channel. The goods carried were mostly expensive luxuries such as wine, weapons and glassware for kings and nobles. As trade increased so did the circulation of money. King Offa began minting silver 'pennies', and the penny remained the basic English coin for centuries afterwards. It was worth much more than the coin we have today. Fourpence or fivepence was enough to buy a sheep.

Both sides of one of King Offa's silver 'pennies'

More about the early English
Later developments in English law are described in Chapter 12.

Books
I. Seraillier (tr.), *Beowulf the Warrior* (O.U.P.). A very readable translation in verse.
Beowulf (Penguin Classics). A clear prose translation.
J. Hamilton and A. Sorrell, *Saxon England* (Lutterworth). Chapters 9–14.
A. F. Titterton, *Homes of the Angles and Saxons* (Ginn's History Bookshelves, Blue Shelf).

Anglo-Saxon farming implements (a scythe blade and a small pickaxe head) and early pottery, dating from around the sixth century

Filmstrips
People of Other Days, Part 5: The Saxons (Visual Publications)

To write and find out
1 Write a short script of an imaginary trial at a Saxon folk-moot, based on the customs described in this chapter. (Aelfric is accused of stealing a cow from Eadric.) Perhaps you can give out the parts and act the scene.
2 Describe a typical day in the life of *either* a churl *or* a churl's wife.
3 In recent years remains of Anglo-Saxon royal halls have been discovered at Yeavering (Northumberland) and Cheddar (Somerset). Try to find out more about them, especially how they were first located and how they were excavated.

5 Justinian and Mohammed

Justinian was one of the greatest Roman emperors. Yet he lived in the sixth century and his palace was nearly a thousand miles from Rome! This may seem strange, but there is a simple explanation. In its later years the Roman Empire was divided into two halves, each with an emperor. The western half grew weak and was finally over-run by barbarians, in the fifth century. But the other half—the lands round the eastern Mediterranean—remained strong and prosperous.

It was this *East* Roman Empire that Justinian ruled, from 527 to 565. His capital was Constantinople, one of the world's richest and best defended cities. It was surrounded by water on three sides, and several stout walls protected the land approach to the city from enemy invasion. Its great harbour, seven miles long, was crowded with ships from many lands.

In the Emperor's magnificent palace, decorated with gold, silver, richly coloured tapestries and mosaics, six regiments of guards pro-tected his sacred person. Justinian considered himself responsible only to God. No man could ever accuse him of making a mistake. Anyone wanting to ask a favour would do so on his knees. However, it was said that Justinian never did anything without taking the advice of his wife—the intelligent and beautiful Empress Theodora. She was the daughter of a circus animal-trainer, and Justinian had to change the law before he could marry a woman of such humble birth.

The conquests of Justinian

As a boy Justinian had learned about the past glories of Rome, in the days when its emperors ruled all the Mediterranean world. His great-est ambition was to recover the western lands lost to the barbarians. He once wrote: 'We have taken hope that the Lord will grant us the rest of the Empire, which the Romans of old . . . lost through idle-ness.' Certainly Justinian was not idle. He worked such long hours that it was said in his court, 'the Emperor never sleeps'.

Justinian began his 'war of reconquest' by attacking the Vandals in North Africa—the weakest of the barbarian kingdoms. In 533 his finest general, Belisarius, set sail with 15,000 troops and landed not far from Carthage. Belisarius's foot-soldiers were fierce fighters, mostly recruited from tribes along the borders of the Empire. His cavalrymen, in their chain-mail coats and iron helmets, were the best in the world. The Vandal army was cut to pieces and, within six months, a large part of North Africa was again a 'Roman' province.

Belisarius next attacked the East-Goths in Italy—Justinian's main goal. Approaching by way of Sicily, he soon captured Rome (537) and Ravenna (540). The war seemed to be won. But the enemy sud-denly recovered, and fighting dragged on until 553, when the Goths were finally defeated. Large parts of Italy suffered great damage.

Mosaic from the church of *San Vitale*, Ravenna, showing the Empress Theodora with her attendants

Rome, which was captured and re-captured several times, became almost a heap of wreckage.

Finally, Justinian's forces moved against the West-Goths in Spain. But after hard fighting they captured only the south-eastern corner of the kingdom. Much of the old Western Empire was still in barbarian hands when Justinian died. However, the Emperor controlled the sea-routes, so at least the Mediterranean was again a 'Roman lake'.

The last emperor to speak Latin

Justinian's wars were very costly, in both money and lives. His subjects were forced to pay crippling taxes for the upkeep of the army. And all the time the Emperor needed extra forces to protect the heart of his empire. The powerful Persians frequently attacked the eastern borderlands; while large sums of gold were paid as bribes to keep back the peoples beyond the Danube frontier.

Despite all his efforts, Justinian's conquests were short-lived. Only a few years after his death most of Italy was overrun by the Lombards. Within a century the foothold in Spain was lost and North Africa was conquered by Arab tribesmen.

Nowadays Justinian is remembered more as a reformer of Roman law than as a conqueror. Over the centuries there had been so many changes in the law that magistrates often did not know what was the correct judgment. So Justinian ordered a team of experts to sort out all that was best in the old Roman laws. The result was the great four-part *Corpus Juris Civilis* (Body of Civil Law) which is still in use today. This vast work fills over 2,000 closely printed pages in a modern edition. It has influenced the laws of many present-day countries in Europe and the Americas.

Justinian is also famous for his buildings—especially the magnificent church of *Santa Sophia* (Holy Wisdom) in Constantinople, which still stands. It took 10,000 men five years to build. The ceiling was overlaid with pure gold, and sunlight flooding through the huge domed roof lit up richly coloured marble floors and walls. A writer of the time said of *Santa Sophia:* 'Whenever one goes there to pray . . . one's heart is lifted up to God and finds itself in heaven.'

The Empire of Justinian, at its fullest extent

Emperors ruled at Constantinople for another 900 years after Justinian. But none of them tried to re-conquer the West. They were

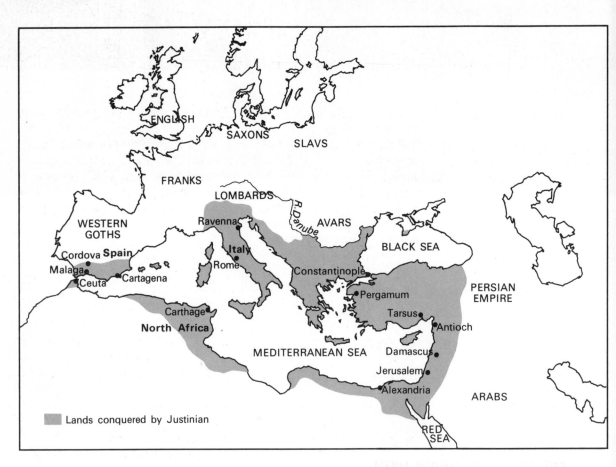

Lands conquered by Justinian

Church of *Santa Sophia* in Istanbul

kept busy defending the empire they already had. As contacts with western Europe grew less the old Roman customs disappeared. Before long even the Christianity of the Eastern Empire was different from that of the Roman Catholic Church. The Empire became known as *Byzantium* — the name of the ancient Greek city which previously stood on the site of Constantinople. Certainly its way of life was Greek rather than Roman. In fact Justinian was the last emperor to speak Latin.

A Prophet from Arabia

Seventy years after Justinian's death the Byzantine Empire was attacked from an unexpected direction. Thousands of armed Bedouins — desert nomads from Arabia — advanced upon the fertile Byzantine lands. This was not the first time that Arabs had left their homeland in large numbers. Arabia is one of the driest and most barren countries in the world. Most of it is desert, scorching hot by day and bitterly cold by night. Any increase in its population meant a shortage of food, and this forced tribesmen to search for richer grazing lands.

But in the seventh century the Bedouins reached much further afield than usual. This was because they were inspired by the religious teachings of a new prophet, who urged them to fight a 'holy war' (*jihad*) to spread the new faith amongst 'unbelievers'. His name was

The Kaaba

Mohammed, and he was born about 570 in the dusty trading town of Mecca. For many years he worked as a merchant, often travelling north to Syria. He probably gained some knowledge of writing and counting in the course of his work.

Mecca was busy with camel caravans. It was also the centre of Arab religion. In its cube-shaped place of worship, called the *Kaaba*, stood statues of several hundred gods—spirits of the stars, rocks, winds and oases. It was a place of pilgrimage where, each spring, pilgrims came from all corners of Arabia to worship in the *Kaaba* and kiss the black stone embedded in one of its walls. This stone, probably a meteorite, was believed to have come from heaven.

The worshipping of many gods and idols troubled Mohammed. He began to retreat to a quiet mountain cave, to think about the question, to fast and to pray for long periods. He said that it was there that the Angel Gabriel appeared to him in a vision and revealed that there was only one god, *Allah*, and Mohammed was to be His Prophet. *Allah* was the same God as the God of the Jews and the Christians. But Mohammed said that the Angel told him he was to be the last in a long line of prophets, including Abraham, Moses and Jesus Christ. These prophets, although bearing the message of God, were not divine.

Camel caravan

Crowds gather round the sacred *Kaaba* in the modern city of Mecca

A mosque, like this one at Isfahan, in Iran (Persia), is a place where Muslims gather to worship *Allah*, under the direction of a prayer leader (they do not have priests)

Mohammed started preaching, but his attacks on the false gods of the Arabs angered the rulers of Mecca. After a time they threatened to silence him. Fortunately the Prophet's fame had spread to Medina 250 miles away. There many Jews and Arabs were attracted by his teachings. So in 622 Mohammed and a few faithful followers moved to Medina. This event, known as the *Hegira* (breaking of old ties) proved such a turning point that it became Year 1 in the Muslim calendar—just as Christ's birth marks the start of Christian times.

The Meccans attacked Medina several times, and fierce battles were fought, during which the Prophet showed himself to be an able military commander. When the Prophet finally captured Mecca in 630 he destroyed the idols in the *Kaaba*, but not the building itself. He pardoned many of his enemies and as a result many of them became followers of his faith. When Mohammed died, two years later, most Arabs had accepted the new religion of *Islam*—meaning 'obedience to the will of God'. Those who 'obey' are called Muslims.

The Koran
The revelations that came to Mohammed were memorised and written down by his followers. They were put in order under his

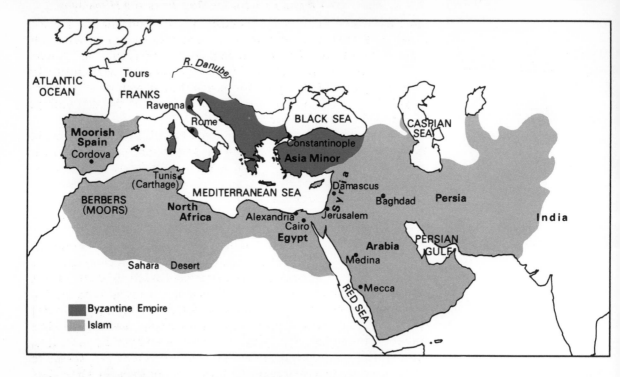

The World of Islam, about
732—a century after the
death of Mohammed

instructions, and compiled in their final form—in a book called the
Koran—less than ten years after the Prophet's death. The text is the
same now as it was then. Nothing has been changed.

The *Koran* is the Holy Book of Muslims. It contains instructions on
how a true Muslim should live his life and how he should worship
God. There are five basic 'Pillars' (rules) of Islam, which Muslims
still follow:

1 The confession of faith: 'There is no God but *Allah* and Mohammed
   is His Prophet.'
2 Prayer: five times a day Muslims pray, facing the *Kaaba* (House
   of God) in Mecca.
3 Fasting: as an act of self-discipline all believers fast from dawn
   to sunset during *Ramadan*, the ninth month of the Muslim year.
4 Charity (*Zakah*): a certain part of a Muslim's income is given to
   the poor and homeless, and other Islamic causes.
5 Pilgrimage (*Hajj*): if possible, every Muslim must make a pilgrimage
   to Mecca once during his lifetime.

The *Koran* also urges believers to struggle for the spread of the
true faith (*jihad*), if necessary by fighting. This 'holy war' was really
aimed at pagans. Islam recognises the faith of the Jewish and
Christian religions and gives them freedom to follow their own
practices.

The *Koran* gave guidance to Muslims in their everyday lives.
For instance, pork was declared unclean and forbidden; gambling
and strong drinks were also forbidden, and the use of faulty weights
and measures in trading condemned. Instructions were given for the
treatment of slaves and the care of wives. The *Koran* said a man may
have up to four wives at any one time, provided he looked after

them all in the same way. This custom arose from the days when there were more women than men, and many of them were left without a protector. The rules regarding divorce were clear. A man had to pronounce publicly 'I divorce you', and the woman had to be allowed to leave the house in peace, taking with her the dowry provided by her family on her marriage. Most of these teachings were based on existing Arab customs.

Mohammed promised to the faithful a Paradise where they might expect to dwell at ease in a 'cool garden of spreading shade, and water gushing, and fruit in plenty'. On the other hand, the 'evil and un-believing' would go to hell, a place of 'scorching wind and scalding water and shadow of black smoke'.

The spread of Islam

United by faith as never before, the Arabs swept northwards conquering the lands of the Byzantine Empire, spreading Islam as they went. Only six years after Mohammed's death (638) Syria was colonised by the Arab armies and thousands of Arabs were making new homes there. Then, turning east, the swift Bedouin horsemen overran the Persian Empire with astonishing ease (637–44). Although Byzantium and Persia had been weakened by long wars against each other, they can hardly have expected their armies to be crushed by poorly-armed tribesmen. Before long Muslims were crossing the frontiers of India and China!

Meanwhile, Egypt was conquered (642) and the Arabs began moving westwards along the North African coast. By 711 Muslim forces were crossing the Straits of Gibraltar into Spain. These were mostly Berbers (or Moors) from the Sahara desert, who had fought hard before accepting the faith of Islam. Now they quickly became masters of Spain, capturing many valuable goods and taking prisoners.

Not until 717 were the armies of Islam seriously checked. Advancing through Asia Minor (now Turkey) they attacked Constantinople by land and sea. But after a bitter struggle the Byzantines forced them back and recovered most of Asia Minor. Soon afterwards the Moors in the West were also checked. They invaded France and had some success at first. But in 732 they were beaten by the Franks, under their leader Charles Martel, the 'mayor of the palace'. Charles Martel, a tough and ruthless warrior, drove the Moors back into Spain, where they remained for a further seven hundred years.

The power of the conquering armies of Islam had passed its peak. But the influence of Islam over the land that stretched from the Atlantic to the Himalayas remained. The Jewish and Christian population had to pay a special tax, but they were allowed freedom of worship. Most of the conquered peoples, however, became Muslims. Apart from Spain, these lands are still largely Muslim today.

After Mohammed's death the Islamic state was ruled by a *caliph* (deputy or successor). From about 750 onwards caliphs had their capital at Baghdad, a great city rivalling Constantinople in its splendour. The caliph Al-Mansur planned the new city of Baghdad as the centre of the still expanding empire. One hundred thousand men built 'the City of Peace' in only four years. The caliphs of Baghdad, however, soon found it impossible to rule the whole of the Islamic world. Distant provinces became self-governing, including Moorish Spain, which was ruled by an *emir* of Cordova.

Merchants and scholars

By breaking down man-made frontiers, Muslims encouraged long-distance trade across three continents. In the crowded *bazaars* (markets) of cities such as Baghdad the rich could buy all manner of luxury goods, many of them unknown in northern Europe. There were jewels, silks, perfumes and spices from China and the Far East; decorated leather and glassware from North Africa and Egypt; furs from central Asia, and magnificent Persian carpets, tapestries and brocades. Arab traders even brought gold, ivory and ostrich feathers from tropical Africa, making the first real contacts between Negro peoples and the outside world.

Helped by the common language of Arabic, ideas travelled as easily as goods throughout Islam. The Arabs had conquered some highly civilised peoples and were quick to learn from them. Great writings from far and wide, especially those of ancient Greece, were translated and stored in vast libraries. Through trading with the Far East, Arabs learned about paper-making, the windmill, spinning wheel and magnetic compass.

These inventions later reached Europe, through Spain and Sicily. So did the nine 'Arabic' numerals that we still use today (they originally came from India). Even more important is the zero, which allows numerals to be arranged in columns representing tens,

Part of the interior of the beautiful *Selimyie* Mosque in Nicosia, Cyprus

Part of Baghdad today

hundreds and so on. Possibly the Chinese first thought of the zero, but it was a ninth century Muslim, Al-Khawarizmi, who first described it in a book that has come down to us. He was also one of the inventors of algebra (*al-jabr* in Arabic).

Not only in mathematics but also in medical science Muslim scholars were far in advance of Europeans in the Middle Ages. They made important discoveries in the treatment of eye disorders, so common in the East. Al-Razi from Baghdad (865–925) wrote about 140 books on medicine, including the first scientific account of smallpox. Avicenna, who lived a century later, wrote a medical encyclopaedia which was the most complete collection of medical knowledge made anywhere in the Middle Ages.

Caliphs themselves often encouraged the work of scholars, poets, artists and musicians. Harun Al-Rashid (caliph 786–809) once gave 5,000 gold pieces, a horse and ten slave girls to a poet who wrote a sonnet in his honour. Needless to say, his reign is famous for its literature! Harun is the hero in many tales of the *Arabian Nights*, a collection of about two hundred stories of fantasy and adventure.

More about Byzantium and Islam
The worlds of Byzantium and Islam form the setting for the later Crusades (see Chapter 13).

Books
A. Powell, *The Rise of Islam* (Longman, Great Civilizations series).
J. D. Bentley, *Byzantium and Justinian* (Hulton, Round the World Histories).
H. O. A. McWilliam, *Muhammad and the World of Islam*, (Longman, Then and There series).
T. T. Rice, *Byzantium* (Rupert Hart-Davis, Young Historian Books).
T. Cairns, *Barbarians, Christians and Muslims* (C.U.P.)
J. C. Allen, *Mohammed and the Rise of Islam* (Hulton, Round the World Histories).
E. R. Pike, *Mohammed* (Weidenfeld and Nicholson, Pathfinder Biographies).
Riadh el Droubie, *Islam* (Longman, Religious Dimension series).
The Koran (Penguin Classics, and Dent, Everyman series).

To write and find out
1 What do you think were the main differences between Christ and Mohammed as men? In what ways were they similar?
2 A pagan camel-driver and a new convert to Islam meet on the road to Mecca ten years after Mohammed moved to Medina. They begin to talk about the recent changes in Mecca, and disagree about whether what has happened is good or not. Imagine and recount their conversation.
3 In which parts of the world is Islam still the chief religion today? Mark these areas on a blank outline map, and compare it with the map in this chapter. (You will need a suitable atlas. One of the best is R. Roolvink, *Historical Atlas of the Muslim Peoples*, published by Allen and Unwin.)

6 Charlemagne, King of the Franks

Bronze statue of Charlemagne

It was the Franks who finally halted the advance of Islam in the West. At the battle of Tours (732) Charles Martel's heavily armed cavalry crushed the Muslim invaders. But away from the battlefield the Franks (who gave their name to France) had much to learn from their opponents.

For centuries to come the Christian peoples of the West were backward in comparison with their Muslim rivals. While the subjects of Islam grew rich through trade, constructed fine buildings and brought together knowledge from many lands, the Franks and their neighbours were mostly ignorant farming folk. They lived simple lives in small isolated villages; knowing nothing of prosperous cities such as Baghdad, Damascus and Cordova.

With the exception of a few monks and priests, knowledge of reading and writing had almost died out among the Franks. In the sixth century, Bishop Gregory of Tours admitted he could not write Latin properly. Yet he took on the task of writing an early *History of the Franks* because he knew of no scholar 'sufficiently skilled in the art of writing' who could do it better! There was little improvement in the next 200 years. Royal documents from this period, written in an ugly scrawl, show that even the king's clerks did not know the simplest rules of grammar.

The palace school at Aachen

The powerful Frankish kingdom was still very backward when Charles Martel's grandson became king in 768. He was also called Charles, but his outstanding achievements soon earned him the name *Charlemagne* (Charles the Great). The new king was strong and athletic, with a firm stride and a commanding voice. He loved riding, hunting or swimming, and, above all, he was a brave and skilful warrior. However, there was another, unusual, side to Charlemagne. He greatly enjoyed study and the company of scholars. Even at his dining table he listened thoughtfully to musicians, poets, or servants reading stories from history.

It shocked the King to find that many priests were so ignorant of Latin that they could neither write properly nor understand the Bible. He was not a scholar himself, but he believed it was a Christian ruler's duty to educate his subjects. To set an example he started a school in his favourite palace at Aachen.

As teachers in the school Charlemagne wanted the best educated men of his day. This meant getting them from other countries— from Italy, Spain and, of course, England, where the scholars of Northumbria had earned a fine reputation. To the King's great delight Alcuin, master of York cathedral school, was persuaded to come to the King's court and organise the teaching there.

Most pupils at the palace school were young men preparing to be priests. Their main studies were the Scriptures and the works of early Christian leaders. But first they were given a good grounding in Latin grammar. For this Alcuin and his companions had to write their own textbooks. At that time there were no books in the Frankish tongue, and most writings of the ancient Greeks were unknown in the West. So all studies in language and literature were narrowed down to Latin.

Naturally Charlemagne wanted many more schools in his kingdom. 'Let every monastery and every abbey have its school', he announced, 'where boys may be taught the psalms . . . singing, arithmetic and grammar.' Charlemagne was thinking of ordinary boys as well as those training to be monks or priests. But that was too much to hope for. The ignorant Franks could not become an educated people overnight. In his lifetime Charlemagne could not expect to do more than improve the education of priests and clerks working in the King's service.

Alcuin of York

Alcuin was an experienced and gifted teacher. He inspired his pupils with a real love of learning. In future years some of them excelled their master and helped to make Frankish scholarship famous in Europe. Besides teaching, Alcuin composed poems, wrote explana

Alcuin

An example of *minuscule* writing

tions of the Scriptures and joined in many discussions with his fellow scholars and the King.

At Charlemagne's request Alcuin also corrected mistakes which over the years had crept into Frankish copies of the Bible and service books. Such errors were often due to carelessness. But sometimes the writing was so bad that copyists in the monasteries could not read it. Alcuin tried to prevent future mistakes by encouraging the use of a neat style of writing called *minuscule*. It was small yet very clear, and it became the basis of most later writing styles.

Charlemagne and Alcuin urged monks throughout the kingdom to make fresh copies of books that were worn or damaged. As a result many priceless manuscripts were saved. Some classic works of the ancient world have come down to us through a single copy made in a Frankish monastery.

After fifteen busy years in Charlemagne's household, Alcuin retired and became abbot of a monastery at Tours. He died there eight years later (804). Alcuin was 'the most learned man of his day', according to Einhard, a leading Frankish scholar. Einhard went to Aachen as a pupil and did so well that he became the King's secretary. He later wrote a *Life of Charlemagne*, which is one of the best biographies of the Middle Ages.

Einhard tells us that the King kept a '. . . writing book under the pillow of his couch, so that when he had time he might practice his hand in forming letters; but he made little progress in this task . . . begun too late in life'. Nevertheless, with the help of his great friend Alcuin, Charlemagne was more successful in other directions. He could work out the dates of movable Church festivals such as Easter; he understood some astronomy and, according to Einhard, he '. . . took great pains to learn foreign languages, gaining such knowledge of Latin that he could make a speech in that language'.

Frankish knights ready for battle

Soldier of Christ

Like most kings called 'Great', Charlemagne was successful in war. Nearly every summer his armies were in action somewhere along the

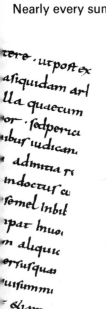

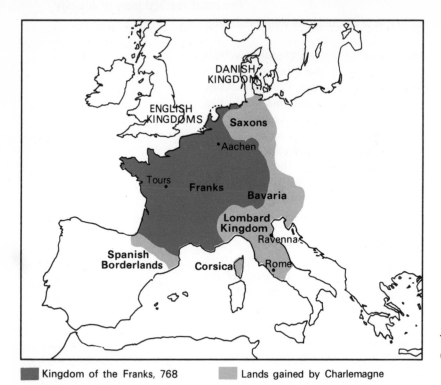

■ Kingdom of the Franks, 768   ■ Lands gained by Charlemagne

borderlands of his kingdom. He did not fight just for glory. Across his frontiers to the north and east were pagan peoples who often raided Frankish territory. In the south were the Muslims of Spain. Charlemagne believed he was doing the work of God by defeating these enemies and gaining new lands for the Christian Church.

In the spring, when the grass was long enough to feed cavalry horses on the move, Charlemagne called up his forces. He could not afford to keep a regular army. His soldiers were mostly landowners— knights on horseback. Each man brought his own weapons. Knights had lances, heavy swords and sometimes bows and arrows, which they fired from the saddle. They acted as a 'shock weapon', breaking up the enemy ranks with a swift charge. After that the heavily armed Franks usually had the advantage in hand-to-hand combat.

Charlemagne called himself 'Defender of the Holy Church'. Like his father, Pepin, he believed it was his duty to protect the Pope. So when the Lombards besieged Rome, early in his reign, Charlemagne led an army over the Alps. He completely destroyed the Lombard kingdom and gave back to the Pope lands he had received from Pepin. The Frankish frontier now lay well to the south of Rome.

Charlemagne had a much tougher struggle against the pagan Saxons. He found it was no use just defeating them in battle, because when his back was turned they rebelled and attacked his kingdom. Charlemagne decided that to get lasting peace he would have to convert them to Christianity—by force if necessary. So he marched into Saxony, and even before the din of battle had died down his missionaries were ordered to begin their work. Those who refused to be baptised were put to death!

Thus Charlemagne fought a 'holy war' against unbelievers, just as Mohammed had done. And sometimes the Frankish King was more ruthless than the Muslims. Einhard tells us that in 782, after a Saxon revolt, 4,500 of the ringleaders were rounded up '. . . and by the King's command they were all beheaded in one day'.

Alcuin protested against converting people at swordpoint, even though it was effective in ending Saxon resistance. Later in his reign Charlemagne allowed more peaceful methods to be used among the Avars in Bavaria. The Franks defeated them in 791 and advanced the frontier far to the east. Over the years the Avars had collected a vast hoard of plunder. This went straight into the Frankish treasury.

Charlemagne was less successful against the Moors of Spain. On his first campaign against them (778) he suffered a serious defeat when the rearguard of his army was ambushed in the Pyrenees (the mountains along the border between France and Spain). After fighting the Moors on and off for twenty years, Charlemagne had to be content with a small strip of territory just beyond the Pyrenees.

Crowned by the Pope

Charlemagne's conquests almost doubled the size of his kingdom. He was by far the most powerful ruler western Europe had known since the days of the Roman Empire. So it seemed fitting that he

The coronation of Charlemagne, as shown in a fourteenth century French chronicle

should be proclaimed 'emperor' over all the lands he governed. This happened, unexpectedly, on Christmas Day, 800. The King was in Rome, so he attended mass at St Peter's Church. After the service the Pope, Leo III, drew near and placed a crown on Charlemagne's head. The congregation cheered and hailed him as 'Emperor of the Romans'.

No doubt Charlemagne was pleased to have the title. Yet afterwards he said the coronation came as a complete surprise to him. 'If he had known the Pope's intention', wrote Einhard, 'he would not have entered the church on that day.' Whether this was true or not, Charlemagne and Leo certainly had different ideas of what the coronation meant. Leo thought he had *given* the title to Charlemagne. But the King refused to accept that the Pope had any authority over him. He was used to telling popes what to do and it was he who gave the orders to the Frankish clergy.

In 813, the year before he died, Charlemagne himself crowned his son Louis—the future emperor of the Franks. The coronation took place not in Rome but at Aachen, in the heart of Frankish territory. This was his way of showing the Pope who was master.

People liked to think that the old Roman Empire had been restored. But Charlemagne's empire was a rather poor imitation. It was much smaller and hardly 'Roman' at all. In fact it was simply an enlarged Frankish kingdom. Charles ruled it just as he had always done, with the help of his nobles and bishops. In each district a *count* kept law and order, collected taxes and, when necessary, called men to arms. To check that counts did their job properly Charlemagne sent out his own 'Messengers of the King'. These travelled in pairs (one of them a churchman, usually a bishop) and they '. . . gave justice to all . . . rich and poor'.

The King, too, was often on the move, going round the empire to make sure his commands were obeyed. Consequently he had no fixed capital, although he spent more time at Aachen than anywhere else. This personal kind of government worked well under a strong and forceful emperor such as Charlemagne. But under weaker rulers the empire soon broke up.

The beginnings of Germany and France

It was a custom among the Franks that when a man died his lands were divided among his sons. Kings were no exception. As it happened both Charlemagne and his son Louis outlived their brothers and were able to rule alone. But when Louis died (840) he left three sons—Lothar, Louis and Charles (nicknamed 'the Bald').

To keep the empire together Louis wanted his eldest son, Lothar, to become sole emperor, and the younger brothers to rule as lesser kings. But Louis and Charles the Bald refused to accept this and civil war broke out. Finally, the three brothers signed a treaty at Verdun (843) by which the empire was divided between them.

The break up of Charlemagne's lands had begun. Soon there were further sub-divisions. However, the rough shapes of the later French and German nations could be seen in two of the kingdoms set up at Verdun. France grew out of the lands given to Charles the Bald, and

The division of
Charlemagne's Empire
by the Treaty of Verdun
(843)

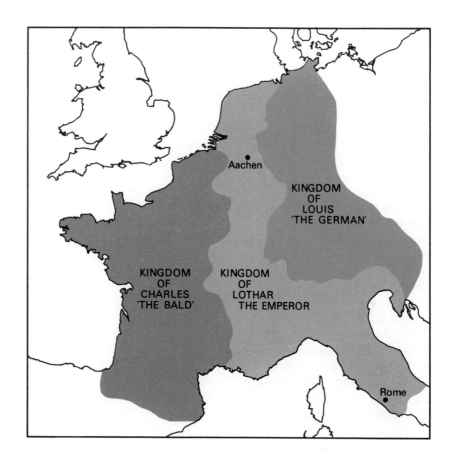

the language of his subjects was the basis of modern French. The kingdom of Louis also had its own language (Old High German) and it later became part of the country we call Germany.

Meanwhile the final collapse of Charlemagne's empire was hastened by enemy attacks from all sides. Muslims raided the Mediterranean coastlands; savage nomad horsemen called Magyars advanced from the plains of Hungary, and from northern Europe came the merciless and destructive Vikings. Towns were burned, churches and abbeys ransacked, and large areas of farming land destroyed. The royal armies could not be everywhere at once. So people looked for protection not to their king, but to their local count.

The popes, too, found that the Frankish rulers were no longer able to protect them. In 959 Pope John XII turned for help to Otto I, a powerful Saxon king from Germany. Otto marched into Italy, defeated the Pope's enemies, and then asked for his reward. He got it early in 962, when John crowned him *Holy Roman Emperor* in St Peter's Church. The Holy Roman Empire was much smaller than that of Charlemagne. It never included more than Germany and North Italy. Yet it lasted until the early nineteenth century.

While Germany grew strong under Saxon kings, France was split up into a number of separate states, ruled by dukes and counts. The last

Tenth century ivory plaque
showing the Emperor
Otto I (seated)

of Charlemagne's descendants died in 987, and the crown was given
to Hugh Capet, one of the nobles. Slowly but surely his family, the
Capetians, built up a new kingdom. It was 200 years before France
had a really powerful king, who could control the nobles and defeat
outside enemies. He was Philip II, and he enters our story in Chapter 13.

More about Charlemagne

Books

D. Dymond, *Charlemagne* (Hutchinson Educational, Men of Mark
   series).

T. Cairns, *Barbarians, Christians and Muslims* (C.U.P.)

R. Winston, *Charlemagne* (A Cassell Caravel Book). For reference,
   especially the illustrations.

To write

1 Give as many reasons as you can why it would have been difficult
   to fight wars in winter in the time of Charlemagne.
2 Charlemagne, like Mohammed, aimed to 'spread the faith by the
   sword'. Write an imaginary conversation in which Alcuin criticises
   the King for his treatment of the Saxons and Charlemagne tries to
   defend his actions.
3 Why did Latin continue to be so important after the fall of the
   Roman Empire?

7 The Vikings and Alfred the Great

One day in June 793 monks on the 'Holy Island' of Lindisfarne noticed some strange ships coming towards them. They had carved figureheads and brightly coloured sails as well as oars. The ships landed and out leapt a band of fierce warriors wearing shirts of chain-mail and metal helmets. Armed with swords and battle-axes, the raiders attacked the surprised monks. They ransacked and burned the monastery and its church, and slaughtered some cattle to re-stock their ships with meat. Then they sailed away with their plunder, before help could come from the mainland of Northumbria.

These mysterious sea-raiders came from the Scandinavian lands of northern Europe. In their language a *vikingr* was a pirate, and to go *a-viking* meant an adventure overseas. This is how they got their name; although some of their victims called them simply 'Northmen'. Undefended monastery churches, with gold candlesticks, cups and other valuable ornaments, were obvious targets for these heathen pirates. They were back in 794 to ransack the church at Jarrow. In the next year St Columba's monastery on Iona was plundered.

All over the country people prayed: 'From the fury of the Northmen, Good Lord deliver us'. But these raids were just a start. For more than 200 years no part of the coasts of western Europe was safe from the merciless Vikings. Whenever the striped sails of their ships appeared on the horizon people fled in terror.

Remains of the west front of Lindisfarne priory, scene of the Viking raid in 793. In the distance Lindisfarne Castle can be seen

Masters of the seas

It was the skill of the Vikings as sailors and the excellence of their ships that made them such deadly enemies. They could strike without warning at any point along thousands of miles of coastline.

Viking ships were a great improvement on the rowing galleys that carried the English settlers to Britain. Each had a proper keel, or 'backbone', made of a single length of oak. This gave sufficient strength to stand the strain of a mast and a large square sail. The *steer-board,* or rudder, was shaped like the blade of an oar and fixed on the right-hand side of the hull, near the stern. This side of a ship

is still called the starboard (from steer-board).

A few well preserved Viking ships have been discovered. Perhaps the best example was found in 1880, under a burial mound at Gokstad, near Oslo. A thick layer of blue clay had kept out water and thus saved most of the wood from rotting. The 'Gokstad ship' was buried about A.D. 900. It is only ten feet longer than a cricket pitch, yet it was able to ride the great Atlantic waves. Although it had a sail its main power came from sixteen oars on each side, which fitted through holes in the oak hull. The total crew was about forty or fifty—all warriors as well as oarsmen.

The seaworthiness of these graceful vessels was shown in 1893, when an exact copy of the Gokstad ship was sailed across the Atlantic, from Norway to Newfoundland. Under sail, speeds of

The Gokstad ship, now in a Norwegian museum. Its owner had been buried in it, along with food, drink, pots and pans, a sledge, and other things it was thought he would need on his journey to the afterworld

ten or eleven knots were reached, and the crossing took only 28 days. The ship came through several storms undamaged. Its captain, Magnus Andersen, praised its excellent steering and the way its springy sides bent with the waves.

The Vikings were not just cruel ruffians. In some ways they were more advanced than their southern neighbours. At a time when most European sailors kept within sight of land, Vikings could steer directly across open sea. They set their course by the position of the sun, or the pole-star after dark. If they met storms or fog they drifted aimlessly, but when the sky cleared they could correct their course. These skilful and adventurous men were among the greatest sailors the world has known.

The voyages of the Norsemen

There were three main Viking races—Norwegians, Danes and Swedes. Most of the sea-raids on Europe were made by Norwegians and Danes. The Swedes were mainly interested in trade. Swedish merchants crossed the Baltic Sea and travelled up the great rivers of Asia and eastern Europe. Some settled round the shores of the Black Sea and traded with the Byzantines and Arabs. These peoples called them *Rus,* and that is how Russia got its name.

The earliest raids on Britain were made by the Norwegians, or 'Norsemen'. They left their coastal *fjords* (creeks) in the spring and returned with the west winds of autumn. Plunder was not their only aim. They were also searching for new places to live. Good farming land is scarce in mountainous Norway, and at this time there was probably a rise in the population.

About the year 800, Norsemen began to settle on the treeless islands to the north and west of Scotland: the Shetlands, Orkneys, Faroes and Hebrides. They brought their families and lived by farming, fishing and seal-hunting. These islands were ideal bases for attacks on Ireland. By 820, according to an Irish chronicle, '. . . there was no harbour or landing-place . . . without fleets of Vikings'. From Ireland, Norse farmers settled in the Isle of Man and parts of north-western England. Some married Celtic women and were converted to Christianity.

Lonely Iceland was the next place to be settled by Norsemen. Although it was too cold for growing grain crops it had grassy regions suitable for cattle and sheep. By about 950 a large Viking colony had grown up there. Present-day Icelanders are descended mainly from these settlers and the Irish women and slaves they took with them.

Later *sagas* (stories) of the Icelanders describe further voyages they made across the unknown Atlantic Ocean. In 982 a tough Norseman called Eric the Red (he had red hair) killed a man and was banished from Iceland for three years. He spent the time exploring a snow-covered land to the west, which had earlier been sighted by fishermen. After much searching he found a few areas of grassland along the coast.

When Eric returned to Iceland he called this new country 'Green-land'. He thought people would want to go there if it had an attractive

SHIP DEVELOPMENT
fifth to ninth centuries

'NYDAM ship'
type used by Saxon raiders
(built about AD400)
—see chapter 1.

Reconstruction of 'SUTTON HOO ship'
early English type
(built about AD600)
—see chapter 1.

'GOKSTAD ship'
Viking type (built about AD850)

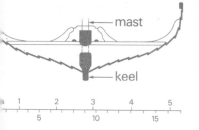

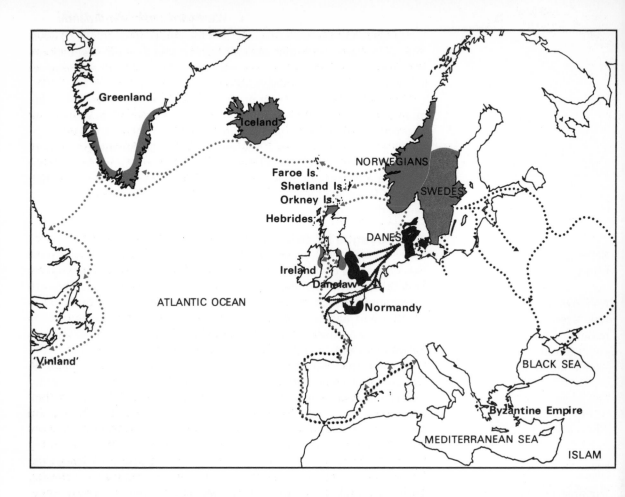

Viking voyages and
conquests, ninth and
tenth centuries

name! Sure enough, when Eric went back to Greenland he was
followed by shiploads of settlers. They must have been disappointed
when they found it was not green at all, but mostly white with snow
and ice. Nevertheless they stayed on, and other settlers followed.
Archaeologists have unearthed some of their stone dwellings,
thickly covered with turf to keep out the biting cold.

According to a saga written in the twelfth century, a man called
Bjarni lost his way while sailing to Greenland in 986. Three times he
sighted a strange coast, where trees grew in large numbers. But
because it was not like reports he had heard of Greenland he went on,
without landing, until he found his destination. If this story is true
Bjarni was the first white man to see the American continent, 500
years before the famous voyage of Columbus.

The saga tells us that a few years later (about A.D. 1000) Leif
Ericsson, son of Eric the Red, decided to go and explore this new
country. Using Bjarni's information to set his course, Leif came to
a land covered with dense forest. Then, sailing southwards into
warmer regions, he came to a pleasant spot where grape-vines grew
wild. 'There was no frost during the winter, and the grass did not
wither very much . . . Leif named the country after its fruits and
called it Vinland [Wineland].'

Coin showing Alfred the Great

Part of the ruins of Hvalsey Church, built by Vikings in Greenland

This seemed an ideal place for Norse settlement. Several expeditions followed, and landings were made along hundreds of miles of the North American coast. But as far as we know all attempts to establish settlements failed, because of attacks by people the Norsemen called *Skraelings.* These were probably Red Indians.

At present archaeologists are searching for evidence to back up the Icelandic sagas. In Newfoundland they have unearthed a group of dwellings similar to those found in other Viking settlements. Nearby they have found evidence of iron-making, which experts have dated to the eleventh century. This is very exciting, because we know that neither Red Indians nor Eskimos were then able to make iron.

Danish attacks

At the time of the early Norse settlements around the British Isles, Danish Vikings were spreading panic in France, Germany and eastern England. At first they plundered coastal villages and monasteries. Then they grew bolder and sailed up great rivers, including the Rhine, Seine and Loire, bringing destruction deep into the heart of the countryside. In 845 a large Danish fleet sailed nearly 200 miles up the Seine to ransack Paris. Soon almost every Frankish town had been destroyed. Parts of North Germany suffered a similar fate. And in the years 859–62 a mixed band of Vikings sailed south, rounded Gibraltar and raided the Mediterranean coast as far as Italy.

The first big Danish attack on England was in 835, when they plundered the Isle of Sheppey, in the Thames estuary. During the next thirty years Danes raided some part of England almost every summer. We are told that there was not a single church left standing within a day's ride of the sea. It was just a matter of time before the fertile soil of England was invaded by these land-hungry Vikings. This happened in the autumn of 865, when a Danish 'Great Army' landed in East Anglia.

The invaders rounded up horses and swiftly conquered most of eastern England. The ruling families of Northumbria and East Anglia were massacred, and their kingdoms came to an end. Dozens of monasteries were destroyed, together with their precious books. Late in 871 the Great Army set up a base near Reading and prepared to attack Wessex—the strongest English kingdom. If the West Saxons were defeated the whole country would be at the mercy of the Danes.

Alfred versus Guthrum

King Ethelred and his brother Alfred led the men of Wessex straight into the attack. They failed to storm the Danish stronghold at Reading, but when the enemy advanced into open country they defeated them in a great battle on the Berkshire Downs. It is said that the King was praying for victory as the Danes drew near. He refused to be interrupted, so Alfred had to start fighting without him! The Danes quickly recovered and evened the score a fortnight later, but they were unable to press home their victory.

Ethelred died suddenly in April 871, leaving the kingdom and all English hopes in the hands of his brother. Alfred was only twenty-

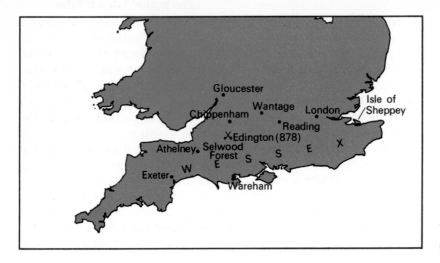

The scene of Alfred's struggles against Guthrum

two, yet he was already a tough and experienced soldier. Throughout the summer the bitter struggle continued, but neither side was able to get on top. Altogether, nine battles were fought in 871. Both armies were exhausted, so they agreed to make peace. Alfred bribed the Danes with money to leave his kingdom. They rode off towards London and five years went by before they returned to Wessex.

In the meantime the Danes attacked Mercia and drove its king, Burgred, across the seas. Wessex had lost its last ally. Part of the Great Army then gave up fighting. By 876 they had shared out a large area of Northumbria and settled down to farm the land.

The rest of the Danes made a fresh attack on Wessex. Under their leader, Guthrum, they rode straight to Wareham, on the Dorset coast. Perhaps they aimed to meet reinforcements coming by sea. But if this was the plan it failed, because 120 Viking ships were lost in a great storm. Guthrum now decided to avoid an open battle. After a long stay in Exeter he left Wessex and made camp at Gloucester (877). A second group of Danish warriors broke away and settled on the lands of eastern Mercia.

If Alfred thought the danger was over he was mistaken. Early in January 878 Guthrum made a surprise raid on Wessex. His army was smaller than before but it caused panic among the West Saxons, who were still enjoying the Christmas festivities. Caught unprepared, many of them surrendered or fled across the Channel. Alfred had no army—only a bodyguard of about 200 thanes and other followers. He retreated into the thick forest of Selwood, and then to the Somerset marshes. There the King established a stronghold, on the 'island' of Athelney, a patch of dry ground rising above the surrounding swamps and thickets.

In later years men made up stories about Alfred's adventures during the dark days of retreat. It was said that the King disguised himself and accepted shelter in a peasant's hut. One day the peasant's wife was cooking some loaves, while Alfred sat by the hearth. 'But when the angry housewife saw the loaves she had set by the fire burning, she rushed up and moved them . . . saying "You wretch,

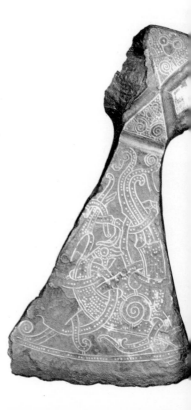

Part of a Danish battle-axe

you're only too fond of them when they're nicely done; why can't you turn them when you see them burning?" '

Spring came, and Alfred sent messengers to his thanes in the nearby shires. They were ordered to arm themselves, gather their followers, and be ready for a signal to meet the King at a secret place. Early in May Alfred left Athelney and joined up with three or four thousand men from Somerset, Wiltshire and Hampshire. The deciding battle was about to be fought.

Guthrum's army waited below the northern edge of Salisbury Plain, at Edington. In the pale light of dawn, Alfred's men formed a shield wall and charged down the grassy slopes. The Danes fought furiously with their two-handed axes, but they were outnumbered and finally forced to retreat. The West Saxons chased them for fifteen miles, to the Danish camp at Chippenham. After a fortnight's siege Guthrum surrendered. The conquests of the Great Army were at an end.

Danish settlements

Peace was made and the Danes promised to leave Wessex for good. Guthrum was baptised a Christian, with Alfred as his godfather. Then he led his men across the country to East Anglia, where they settled peacefully to plough the land and sow crops.

Alfred was now the real ruler of all Englishmen living outside the Danish settlements. In 886 he made another pact with Guthrum,

Danish settlements in the ninth century

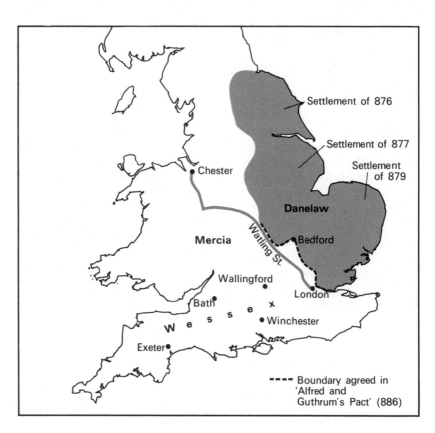

which fixed a frontier between the English lands and the *Danelaw*, where Danish laws and customs were followed. The frontier went . . . up the Thames, and then up the River Lea to its source, then straight to Bedford, and up the River Ouse to Watling Street' (the old Roman road). 'Alfred and Guthrum's Pact' also forbade cattle stealing across the frontier, and declared that 'If a man be killed, whether an Englishman or a Dane, we shall all place the same value [wergeld] on his life'.

The English living within the Danelaw seem to have been fairly treated. Most Danes cleared new land for themselves instead of driving the English from their homes. The names of Danish settlements have endings such as -by, -thorp or -thorpe (meaning village) and -toft (homestead). Some of these are important towns today— for instance Grimsby, Scunthorpe and Lowestoft. In Lincolnshire, where Danish place-names are most common, some country folk still call a farmhouse the 'toft'.

Although the threat of the Great Army was over, Alfred decided to strengthen his defences in case of future attack. Round the borders of Wessex he built a number of strongholds called *burhs* (this is where the word 'borough' comes from). Some burhs were built at places like Exeter, Bath and Winchester, where the remains of old Roman walls could be patched up. But in most cases new earthen banks and ditches had to be made.

Alfred also started building warships. They had sixty oars and were nearly twice as long as Danish ships. But it would be a long time before English sailors could match the skill of the Vikings. As well as building a navy, Alfred re-organised his army. Men had always disliked leaving their fields unattended just when it was time for sowing or harvesting. So in future only *half* the total force would have to fight. The other half would carry on farming. After a certain time the two halves changed places.

The new West Saxon defences were soon put to the test. In 892 a large force of Danes crossed the Channel from France and landed on the Kent coast. In the next four years they plundered many parts of the Midlands and south-eastern England, living on stolen crops and slaughtered cattle. But most of Alfred's burhs held firm. The invaders were finally defeated and forced to split up. Some settled in the Danelaw and the rest sailed back to try their luck in France.

England now enjoyed a long period of peace. But Viking raids against the weak Frankish kingdom went on unchecked. In 911 the French king, Charles 'the Simple', realised he could not get rid of the invaders and decided to come to terms with them. He invited a Viking chieftain named Rollo to become the lawful duke of the lands he controlled at the mouth of the River Seine. In return Rollo had to promise to protect Charles against further raids.

Rollo and his followers were rough seafaring men. But once they settled down they quickly became more civilised. They mixed with the Franks, who converted them to Christianity and taught them to speak French. The 'Duchy of the Northmen' became known as Normandy. It grew bigger and more powerful. Chapter 9 tells how a later Norman duke became King of England in 1066.

Wallingford, on the banks of the river Thames. This was one of the largest of Alfred's *burhs*. The dotted line marks the position of the original Saxon bank and ditch

Timeline

A.D.	
793	Viking attack on Lindisfarne
865	Danish 'Great Army' lands in England
871–99	Alfred 'the Great' King of Wessex
878	Alfred defeats Guthrum at Edington
911	Normandy founded by Rollo
about 1000	Leif Ericsson lands in North America

More about the Vikings

Further achievements of Alfred in peacetime are described in the next chapter. Books on Alfred are also listed in Chapter 8.

Books

G. L. Proctor, *The Vikings* (Longman, Then and There series).

J. D. Bentley, *Leif Ericsson and the North Atlantic* (Hulton, Round the World Histories).

C. A. Burland, *The Vikings* (Hulton Educational).

A. Boucher, *A Viking Raider* (O.U.P., People of the Past).

M. E. Reeves, *Alfred and the Danes* (Longman, Then and There series). Pages 1–27, 43–44, 54–60.

F. R. Donovan, *The Vikings* (A Cassell Caravel Book). For reference.

Filmstrips

The Vikings (A. B. Europa, distributed by Unicorn Head).

People of Other Days, Part 6: The Vikings (Visual Publications).

Ciné Films

The Vikings: Life and Conquests (Encyclopaedia Britannica, distributed by Rank).

The Vikings (distributed by the Royal Norwegian Embassy).

To write and find out

1 In the style of a modern newspaper report, write an 'eyewitness account' of about 200–300 words on *either* the attack on Lindisfarne (793) *or* Guthrum's attack on Wessex (January 878). At the time Alfred's camp was at Chippenham.

2 Explain the origin of the following names: Russia, Greenland, Vinland, Danelaw and Normandy. Which two of these are no longer used today?

3 How many places can you find with names ending in *-by, -toft, -thorp* or *-thorpe*? Mark them on a blank outline map of England. What does the distribution of dots tell you about the places where Vikings settled?

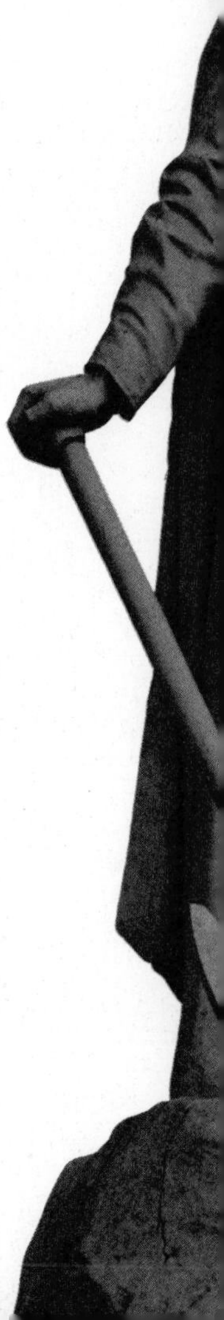

8 The Kingdom of All England

Statue of Alfred at Wantage in Berkshire, where he was born in 849

Alfred the Great is remembered as the king who saved England from the Danes. He defeated them in battle, built warships and strongholds, or *burhs,* for defence, and reformed the army of Wessex. But these military achievements were only part of his life's work. Like Charlemagne, Alfred believed that studying, praying and making good laws were just as important as winning battles.

Alfred – England's schoolmaster

Some time after the defeat of Guthrum, Alfred sent a letter to each of his bishops. Looking back to his childhood, he wrote: 'I remembered how I saw, before everything was ravaged and burnt, that the churches all over England were filled with treasures and books.' But due to the destruction of monasteries and libraries by the Vikings, Alfred went on to say: '. . . when I came to the throne there were very few churchmen . . . who could understand their service books in English or translate even a letter from Latin into English'.

Alfred was determined to restore learning and education in his kingdom. Just like Charlemagne, he invited scholars from home and abroad to his court. One of them was Bishop Asser, a Welshman, who later wrote a *Life of Alfred.* This book tells us a lot about the King. But we have to be careful how we use it because later writers and copyists altered the original text and added bits to it.

Alfred had no schooling in his youth. Like most Anglo-Saxon kings, he was brought up to be a soldier and to love hunting and the 'joys of the hall'. But when he was nearly forty years old he began to learn reading and writing, with the help of Bishop Asser. The King must have studied hard, especially during the long winter evenings, because after about five years he could write fairly good English and Latin.

Up to Alfred's time *Englisc,* as he called it, was mainly a spoken language. Songs, stories and poems were learned and recited, but few seem to have been written down. The laws of kings had to be written in English, because they were for all the people, not just the educated. But books were in Latin – the language of scholars and churchmen.

Now Alfred decided it was time for a change. He wanted to translate certain important books into English. Then the sons of his thanes, who one day would help to govern the kingdom, could be taught to read in 'the tongue we can all understand'. Only those that were 'fit for higher learning' or wanted to be priests would have to study Latin as well.

Among the books translated by the King and his scholars were Gregory the Great's *Pastoral Rule*, Bede's *History of the English Church and People*, and *Universal History*, written by a Roman

⁊ duda ⁊ osmod .ii. ealdormenn forð ferdon · AN·DCCCXXXIIII

Her com micel sciphere on west wealas ⁊ hi to anum gecyrdon
⁊ ƿið ecgbryht ƿest sexena cyng ƿinnende ƿæron þa he þæt ge
hyrde he mid fierde ferde ⁊ him ƿið gefeaht æt hengestes
dune ⁊ ær ge þa flymde ge wealas ge pyhtas ge hade scian.

Her ecgbryht cing forð ferde ⁊ hyne hæfde ær offa mircena
cing ⁊ bryhtric ƿest sexena cing aflymed .iii. gear of angel cynnes
lande on franc land ær he cing ƿære ⁊ þy fultome dbryht ric
offan byhte hæfde his dohtor him to cwene · ⁊ se ecgbryht ric
rode .xxxvii. ƿintra · ⁊ .vii. monað. ⁊ feng þa æþelwulf ecg
bryhting to ƿest sexena rice ⁊ he sealde æþestane his suna
cantwara rice ⁊ east sexena rice ⁊ suð rigea · ⁊ suð seaxena ·

Her wulfheard ealdor mann gefeaht æt hamtune ƿið .xxxiii.
scyphlæsta ⁊ þær micel ƿæl gesloh ⁊ sige nam ⁊ þy geare
forð ferde wulfheard ⁊ þy ilcan geare gefeaht æþelhelm
ealdorman ƿið deniscne here on port mid dorsætum · ⁊ lo
deh ƿile þone here geflymde ⁊ hade scian ahton ƿæl stope
ge ƿeald ⁊ þone ealdormann of slogan.

Her herebryht ealdormann ƿæs of slegen fram hæþenu
mannum ⁊ manige menn mid him on merscwarum ⁊ þy
ilcan geare eft on lindesige ⁊ on east englum ⁊ on cant ƿarum
ƿurdon of slegene fram þam herige.

Her ƿæs micel ƿæl slieht on lundene ⁊ on cantƿara byrig
⁊ on hrofes ceastre. AN·DCCC·XL.

Her æþelwulf cing gefeaht æt carrum ƿið .xxxv. scyp
hlæsta ⁊ þa denis can ahton ƿæl stope ge ƿeald.

AN·DCCCXLII · AN·DCCCXLIII · AN·DCCCXLIIII·

Artist's impression of an English soldier at the time of Alfred

called Orosius in the fifth century. The latter contained geography as well as history, and the translators put in extra bits of information, especially about the geography of northern Europe. Alfred played a large part in all this work. In the front of the *Pastoral Rule* it says: 'King Alfred translated every word of me into English.'

History was one of Alfred's special interests. He got scholars to find out all they could about the history of the English ever since the earliest settlements. Monastery records were collected, and also songs and stories that had been passed from one generation to the next. Then an *Anglo-Saxon Chronicle* was written—a kind of diary, but in years rather than days. For the earlier centuries it is little more than a register of kings and battles. But when it gets to Alfred's time the Chronicle is very detailed.

Copies of the *Anglo-Saxon Chronicle* were sent to a number of monasteries, where they were kept up to date. Seven different versions have been discovered, one of them continuing up to 1154. They all tell much the same story, although occasionally they contradict each other. From Alfred's reign onwards the Chronicles are very accurate, because events were recorded at the time they were happening.

In 899 the chroniclers had sad news to report: 'In this year Alfred son of Ethelwulf died, six days before All Saints' Day . . . he had held the kingdom for one and a half years less than thirty.' The Chronicle itself and Alfred's own writings were his greatest memorial to future ages. He left many fine buildings as well—royal halls, new churches and monasteries. And he restored older churches that had been damaged in the Danish wars or were falling into decay. We also remember Alfred through his Code of Laws. In this he tried to give special protection to his poorer and weaker subjects, who were often harshly treated by powerful landowners. No one summed up Alfred's life better than the King himself, when he wrote: 'I desired to live worthily . . . and to leave after my life . . . my memory in good works.'

Re-conquest of the Danelaw

Alfred's kingdom passed to his son, Edward 'the Elder'. He was an experienced soldier and he set out to increase the power of Wessex. His main aim was to conquer the Danelaw—the lands where the Danes had settled in eastern England. The Mercians, who no longer had a king of their own, fought on Edward's side. They were led by his sister Ethelfleda, who was known as the 'First Lady of the Mercians'.

The English made a two-pronged advance into the Danelaw; Edward from the south and Ethelfleda from the west. Like mice nibbling at cheese they conquered the land in small stages. In each newly-won area a *burh* was constructed, just like those Alfred had built to protect Wessex.

The Danes offered little serious resistance. By this time they had settled down and given up fighting. Most of them were prepared to accept Edward as their king, provided they could go on farming in peace. This suited Edward, because he did not intend to force them off the land. By 920 the conquest of the Danelaw was almost

Left: An extract from the *Anglo-Saxon Chronicle*, which is preserved in the British Museum, London. Here some of the Danish invasions are described— in English very different from that we speak today!

King Athelstan, holding
Bede's *Life of St Cuthbert*

complete. The Danes were converted to Christianity, and churches and monasteries were built, often at places where earlier abbeys had been destroyed by the Great Army.

At the end of Edward's reign (925) all the English in the South and Midlands looked to him as their king. Edward's son Athelstan carried on where his father had left off. He took firm control of northern England, and even invaded Scotland. In 937 Athelstan was attacked by a large force of Scots, Britons and Norse settlers. But he crushed them in a great battle at Brunanburh, somewhere in Northumbria. According to the *Anglo-Saxon Chronicle,* 'Never before on this island . . . was a greater slaughter of a host made by the edge of the sword since the Angles and Saxons came here.'

Athelstan now called himself *Rex Totius Britannae* (King of all Britain) on his coins. His fame as a warrior had already spread far beyond the British Isles. Kings and dukes on the Continent sent him messages of friendship and beautiful gifts of gold and silver ornaments, weapons and decorated books. Athelstan gave richly in return.

Artist's impression of an ealdorman from the late Anglo-Saxon period

Thus the kingdom of England grew out of the kingdom of Wessex. The Danes had helped to make this possible, although they did not realise it at the time. They destroyed the other kingdoms and so cleared the way for the union of all the English under a single king. Several centuries passed before the northern border with Scotland was fixed. But a start was made by King Edgar (959–75). He gave all the lands north of the River Tweed to Kenneth, king of the Scots. The Tweed still forms part of the Border today.

Shires, hundreds and towns

Once the Danelaw was conquered it was divided into *shires*; many of them centred round towns, such as Derby, Nottingham or Leicester. Shires had already been formed in most other parts of England. Some of the southern ones, including Kent and Sussex, began as separate kingdoms. Nowadays we call these local divisions counties. Most of them still have the boundaries that were fixed in Anglo-Saxon times.

Each shire had its law court or *shire moot,* which met twice a year to deal with serious crimes and disputes. It was attended by important landowners, and a royal official called an *ealdorman* was in charge. He was the king's representative in that area. Among his other duties he had to call up and lead the shire forces in wartime.

In return for their service to the king, ealdormen (later called eorls) were given money and large estates. Some became very powerful nobles, controlling several shires at once. Their ordinary duties in each shire were given over to a shire-reeve, or *sheriff.* By the eleventh century one or two eorls were strong enough to challenge the power of the Crown. One of them, Harold Godwine, actually became king for a time in 1066.

Ordinary villagers helped to run affairs in their own district. Shires were divided into smaller areas called *hundreds,* which probably at first contained 100 'hides' or households. In each there was a monthly meeting called the *hundred moot,* where thieves, cattle-rustlers and other criminals were brought to justice. Commands from the king were read out by the leader of the meeting, known as the 'hundred man'.

There were also *burh moots* in the towns. This reminds us that many English towns grew up at places where Alfred, Edward and Ethelfleda built burhs for defence against the Danes. Some of these were quite big. Winchester and Wallingford (see picture in Chapter 7) were each encircled by about two miles of defences.

The protection given by these walled strongholds attracted merchants and craftsmen. They wanted market places where they could store and sell their goods in safety. Other towns grew up at harbours, crossroads, or beside cathedrals and large monasteries. London had long been the main centre of shipping and overseas trade. It received cargoes of wine, fish, timber and pepper; and exported wool, cheese and iron goods. Even in the eighth century Bede had described London as '. . . the market of many nations, coming to it by sea and land'. Canterbury and York, the homes of the two archbishops, were also fairly large settlements at that time.

These places were very different from modern towns. They looked more like overgrown villages, bordered by farmlands where corn grew and cattle grazed. Some town dwellers earned their living from the land. But most were merchants, clerks or craftsmen of some sort. So extra food had to be brought in from the countryside.

One thing that would strike us about Anglo-Saxon towns would be the large number of churches. By the eleventh century there were about twenty in Norwich—roughly one for every 300 people. Churches were built of stone. So were the halls belonging to great nobles. But the houses of ordinary citizens were made of wood and thatch.

Experts can only give a rough estimate of the size of these towns. London was almost certainly the biggest. It probably had a population of more than 10,000 by the eleventh century. York and Winchester were not far behind. Probably each had over 8,000 citizens. Winchester had long been the chief city of Wessex. The king's main treasure was kept there. But it would be wrong to think of Winchester, or London, as the 'capital' of England. The King and his court still travelled around the country, and the Witan could be called to meet on any of the royal estates.

The main towns in England a thousand years ago. Notice that most of these towns grew up in the areas of Danish settlement. The Danes preferred to live in larger communities than the English. Apart from London, none of these towns is among the largest thirty in England today

The return of the Vikings

After the English had enjoyed a century of peace under strong kings, the dreaded dragon-heads of Viking ships were again seen along the coasts. This is how the *Anglo-Saxon Chronicle* described the early raids:

980 . . . Southampton was ransacked by a naval force, and most of the citizens killed or taken captive; and in that same year Thanet was ravaged.

981 . . . great damage was done everywhere by the coast both in Devon and Cornwall.

982 . . . three ships of Vikings arrived in Dorset and ravaged in Portland. That same year London was burnt down.

These attacks were made by quite small groups of adventurers. But before long Scandinavian kings came in person, leading powerful

armies of highly-trained warriors. The English were no match for them, and brave stands at Maldon, in Essex, and London ended in defeat. Things might have been different if there had been another Alfred to defend England. But the land was ruled by a weak king, Ethelred. Nowadays he is remembered as Ethelred 'the Unready', but in fact he was known as the *Unraed,* which meant 'without good advice'.

Instead of fighting, Ethelred collected extra taxes and bribed the invaders to go away with large sums of money called *Danegeld* (Dane-payment). The Viking leaders rewarded their warriors and sailed away. But they were soon back for more! Still Ethelred preferred to pay rather than fight. The *Anglo-Saxon Chronicle* tells us that' . . . when the enemy were in the east, the English army was kept in the west, and when they were in the south, our army was in the north . . . Finally there was no leader willing to collect an army, but each fled as best he could.'

Year after year the Vikings seemed content to come just for *Danegeld.* But finally Swein 'Forkbeard', King of Denmark, decided to conquer England. In 1013 he landed in the North with a large army. Ethelred fled across the Channel and Swein took the crown. But he was only king for a few weeks. He collapsed and fell dead off his horse in February 1014.

Ethelred came back, but he soon faced an army led by Swein's son Cnut (sometimes spelt Canute). By the end of 1016 Ethelred was dead, and so was his son Edmund, who had fought bravely against the invaders. Tired of the struggle, the English accepted Cnut as their king. He was only twenty years old.

King Cnut

Cnut was a strong and courageous young man. But he was sometimes very cruel. He had grown up in a hard world, surrounded by violence and bloodshed. So he did not hesitate to order the deaths of leading Englishmen he could not trust. Cnut's subjects feared him, but in time they also learned to respect him as a king who ruled firmly and justly.

To give himself a link with the English royal family, Cnut married Emma, Ethelred's widow. Then he set out to restore peace. He sent most of his fleet back to Denmark, after paying them off with the largest *Danegeld* ever collected in England—82,500 pounds of silver. Cnut kept forty ships, and also a few of his best soldiers, who became the King's *housecarls* (bodyguards).

Once his position was secure, Cnut called together a great assembly of nobles and Church leaders. He promised to rule fairly and to keep the laws of Edgar (who reigned before Ethelred). Although he gave lands to some of his Danish followers, many English nobles were allowed to keep their estates and positions of power. Cnut also promised to help and protect the Christian faith. True to his word he built fine stone churches and even went on a pilgrimage to Rome in 1027.

For most of his nineteen-year reign Cnut was King of Denmark as well as England. And for a short time he ruled Norway and part of

Coin from the reign of Ethelred. Thousands of these were used to pay *Danegeld*

Sweden too. At least the English were safe from Viking attacks while Cnut reigned! When he died, in 1035, there were two sons to follow him. It seemed his family was well established on the English throne. Yet only seven years later both sons were dead and Cnut's great North Sea empire had broken up.

The English crown went to Edward, son of Ethelred and a descendant of the kings of Wessex. He had grown up in Normandy, where he was taken for safety during Ethelred's reign. Edward knew less about England than the Danish kings he followed. But he was the great, great, great grandson of Alfred. That was enough to win him the support of the people.

King *Cnut,* depicted in an eleventh century manuscript

More about Alfred and the English kingdom
Books

M. E. Reeves, *Alfred and the Danes* (Longman, Then and There series). Pages 28–53, 61–68.

C. Oman, *Alfred, King of the English* (Dent).

M. Fitt, *Alfred the Great* (Nelson, Picture Biographies).

Alfred the Great (Cape, History Jackdaw series, no. 89).

The Anglo-Saxon Chronicle (Everyman's Library). For reference.

Filmstrip

King Alfred the Great (Wills and Hepworth, Adventures from History). For younger children.

To write and find out

1 List the similarities and differences between Alfred the Great and Charles the Great (Charlemagne).

2 What have the Old English words *ealdorman, eorl* and *burh* come to mean in modern English? How do the present-day meanings differ from those of Anglo-Saxon times?

3 Give *two* reasons why the Vikings found England easier to conquer in the eleventh century than in the ninth.

4 No doubt you have heard a story that Cnut once tried to turn back the waves. Where is this supposed to have taken place and what was the outcome?

9   The Norman Conquest

In the French town of Bayeux there is an exhibition gallery near the cathedral. Preserved in a glass frame around its walls is the world's most famous piece of needlework. It is a long strip of tapestry, made about 900 years ago. In a series of seventy-two pictures it shows how Duke William of Normandy conquered England in 1066. We see men feasting, hunting, fighting and dying, castles and ships being built, and action-packed battle scenes.

The pictures have Latin sub-titles. So the Bayeux tapestry is a kind of strip-cartoon and chronicle combined. It was probably made by English women, soon after 1066, at the orders of William's half-brother, Bishop Odo of Bayeux. The pictures were embroidered in eight colours of wool thread on pieces of linen. Then they were sewn together, making one long strip over 230 feet long and $19\frac{1}{2}$ inches wide. A few pictures at the end have been lost. But it is still remarkable that a delicate tapestry should have survived from the eleventh century, while many stone buildings from this period have long since fallen into ruins.

The hero of the story, William 'the Conqueror', was descended from Rollo the Viking, who became the first duke of Normandy in 911 (see Chapter 7). Like his forefathers, William was tough, courageous and had a spirit of adventure. His army was the very last to invade and conquer England. That is why 1066 is a date everyone remembers.

Others have tried to repeat the success of the Normans, but all have failed. As recently as 1940 Hitler planned a German conquest of Britain, but the brave resistance of the R.A.F. stopped him. It was the strength of the Royal Navy that prevented earlier invasions by Napoleon, Emperor of France, in 1804, and Philip II of Spain, who sent his famous Armada in 1588. Napoleon and Hitler commanded vast armies and controlled much of Europe. Yet William of Normandy ruled a small dukedom not much bigger than Wales!

Rivals for the crown

As the year 1065 drew to a close, King Edward of England lay dying in his London palace. His reign of more than twenty-three years had not been a happy one. Edward was a shy, peace-loving man. He lacked the necessary firmness and strength of character to keep control of his powerful nobles. As a young man he gave most of his time to hunting and other idle pleasures. In the later years of his reign he became very religious, spending many hours praying and confessing his sins. To his subjects, Edward, known as 'the Confessor', seemed more like a monk than a king.

The nobles and bishops of the King's Council (or Witan) gathered in London for the Christmas court of 1065. But the festivities were overshadowed by Edward's illness and the big question—who was to

King Edward 'the Confessor', as shown in the Bayeux Tapestry

be the next king? The Confessor had been married for twenty years but had no children. His nephew, also called Edward, had died leaving a son, Edgar. But Edgar was only a child. There was no Englishman of royal blood old enough to be king.

Nowadays we have laws to decide who will be king or queen. When a ruler dies the crown passes automatically to the next in succession. But 900 years ago there were no hard and fast rules. Even if the old king had sons they might be considered too young to rule, and so be passed over in favour of someone else. Often the crown went to the man whom the previous king *designated* (chose to follow him).

The doubts about Edward's successor provided a perfect opportunity for Harald Hardrada, the powerful king of Norway. Everyone knew that before the Confessor's reign England had been ruled by Viking kings—Cnut and his sons. Now Hardrada claimed he was the rightful heir to the throne. When Edward finally died, on 5 January 1066, it seemed certain that England would soon be invaded by the King of Norway.

The English needed a new king quickly, and he would have to be a good soldier. Edward, on his deathbed, had named Harold Godwine, Earl of Wessex, as his successor. Earl Harold was not of royal blood, although his sister, Edith, was the Confessor's queen. But he was the most powerful Englishman and the commander of Edward's army. No one doubted Harold's courage and ability as a soldier, and he had governed his earldom justly and well. Thus, without delay, the Witan confirmed Harold as King. He was crowned on the day of Edward's burial.

When news of this reached Duke William in Normandy he flew into a rage. He claimed that Edward had promised the crown to *him* some years before! This was probably true. Edward had grown up in Normandy, under the care of William's father. He had many Norman friends and advisers in his household. During the winter of 1051-2 William visited England and was welcomed at Edward's court. It is likely that the promise was made at this time.

Why did the Confessor fail to keep his word? In his later years he must have realised that the English nobles would not accept a foreign duke as their king. They often showed strong dislike of Edward's Norman friends and forced some of them to leave the country. So, reluctantly, Edward named the Englishman, Harold—even though he had never liked the Godwine family. On one occasion Harold's father had even rebelled against him.

This was all very well, but it did not stop William from believing he should be king. And he claimed that not only Edward but Harold too had promised to help him get the crown! If this was so it probably happened in 1064. The Bayeux tapestry shows Harold being sent on some kind of mission by King Edward. He landed on the Normandy coast where, to his surprise, he was arrested by the local count and handed over to William. The tapestry shows Harold taking a sacred oath to support the Duke. No doubt this included helping him to get the English throne when Edward died.

We do not know whether Harold took the oath freely. It is likely

Scene from the Bayeux Tapestry showing King Harold at the time of his coronation. It took place at Westminster Abbey church, newly built by the Confessor and opened a few days before his death. Nearly every king has been crowned there since 1066.

that William put pressure on him. If so, Harold did not have to keep his word. Nevertheless, William declared Harold an oath-breaker and ordered his men to prepare for war. He sent messengers to some of his French neighbours, offering them lands in England if they would help him defeat Harold and get the crown.

Victory at Stamford Bridge

At the end of April 1066, a fiery comet appeared in the sky and shone brightly every night for a week. The *Anglo-Saxon Chronicle* tells us that '. . . all over England there was seen in the heavens such a sign as men had never seen before. Some said it was the star "comet" which some call the long-haired star.' Modern astronomers call it Halley's comet and we now know that it appears at fairly regular intervals, usually every seventy-five or seventy-six years. But Englishmen living in 1066 believed it was a sign from the Almighty warning them of dreadful troubles that lay ahead.

On both sides of the Channel preparations for war went on through the summer months of 1066. The Bayeux tapestry shows William's men cutting trees, making boats and loading them with weapons, horses and food. Meanwhile Harold gathered a large army on the south coast and stationed his fleet off the Isle of Wight.

By August William was ready, but he was stopped from sailing because the wind was in the wrong direction. Although he did not realise it this was to his advantage. Harold was fully prepared for the invasion in August. But when it was delayed things began to go wrong

Count Guy of Ponthieu orders his men to seize Harold. We have no idea why Harold landed in Normandy. It is possible that he was aiming for another part of the coast and was blown off course

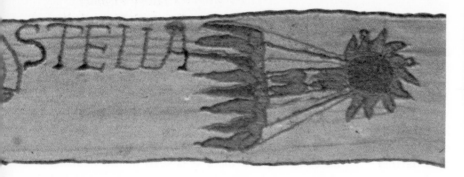
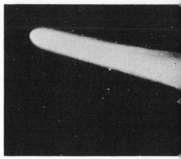

for him. Harvest time was approaching and his soldiers were eager to go home. By early September his food supplies were running out and he was forced to disband his army. At the same time the English fleet was sent from the Isle of Wight to London. On the way many ships were lost in a storm. Now the Channel was undefended.

A few days later Harold received dreadful news. Harald Hardrada, king of Norway, had landed on the north-east coast! The same north wind that kept William's ships in port assisted Hardrada's voyage from the Orkney Islands, where he had gathered men and supplies. With him was Harold Godwine's brother Tostig. He had been banished from his earldom in England the previous year and was now determined to win back his lands by force.

Hardrada and Tostig sailed up the Humber with 200 warships and many smaller craft. They landed a large army and on 20 September won a hard battle near York against the northern earls, Morcar of Northumbria and Edwin of Mercia. But King Harold was already marching north at great speed, gathering an army as he went. By 25 September he was ready to strike.

The *Anglo-Saxon Chronicle* states that 'Harold our king came upon the Norwegians by surprise and met them beyond York at Stamford Bridge . . . few survived and the English remained in command of the field'. Both Hardrada and Tostig were killed, and so great was the slaughter that the survivors needed only 24 ships for their escape!

Defeat at Hastings

Harold had crushed the most feared warrior of the northern world. But his victory celebrations were cut short by messengers bringing news that William had landed on the south coast.

The wind changed two days after the battle of Stamford Bridge. Immediately William's army set sail, and on the morning of 28 September landed on the Sussex coast, at Pevensey. It is said that when William leapt ashore he slipped and covered his hands with sand. 'You've already got a grip on the soil of England, Duke', said one of his knights. William moved his army a short distance along the coast and made camp at Hastings. He ordered his men to build a castle of timber.

Meanwhile, Harold's soldiers began the 250-mile march from York. They were tired and reduced in numbers after the battle of Stamford Bridge. The King reached London to find reinforcements

Left: The Comet as it is shown in the Bayeux Tapestry
Above: Halley's Comet, photographed on 4 May 1910. It is named after Edmund Halley who, in 1704, became the first astronomer to calculate its orbit and establish the fact that it reappears at fairly regular intervals. It is next expected in 1986

Right: The building of William's invasion fleet

hurrying from the surrounding shires. But men from more distant parts did not get there in time. When Harold left London on the final stage of his journey his army of six or seven thousand was disappointingly small. The Norman army was probably smaller, but it was much better equipped. William had many trained knights on horseback, whereas most of Harold's men fought on foot.

Harold halted about nine miles from Hastings and drew up his forces on Senlac Hill, where the village of Battle now stands. It was a good position because the enemy would have to advance up a slope. William immediately moved his army inland and attacked the

NAVIGIO: MAR E TRAN SIVIT

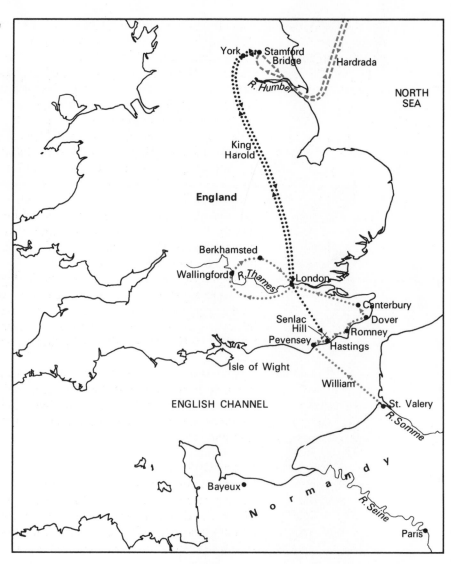

1066: movements of the rival armies

York
Stamford Bridge
Hardrada
R. Humber
NORTH SEA
King Harold
England
Berkhamsted
Wallingford
R. Thames
London
Canterbury
Dover
Senlac Hill
Romney
Pevensey
Hastings
Isle of Wight
William
St. Valery
R. Somme
ENGLISH CHANNEL
N o r m a n d y
Bayeux
R. Seine
Paris

ET VENIT AD PEVENE SÆ :-

hIC EXE

Above: After sailing from St Valery, at the mouth of the river Somme, William's invasion fleet approaches the English coast. Notice the horses on board

English position next day. The battle began at about half-past nine on the morning of Saturday, 14 October.

The two-handed battle-axes of Harold's *housecarls* (bodyguards) were deadly weapons at close quarters. They could knock off a man's head in a single blow. So William's archers kept at a safe distance and fired showers of arrows. Time after time the Norman knights galloped up the hill and tried to scatter the opposition, but the English kept in close formation behind their 'shield wall'.

After several hours of fighting the result was still in doubt. Then the English made a mistake. Part of the Norman army retreated in disorder, tempting many of Harold's men to chase after them. But the Normans recovered quickly and cut down the attackers. This showed how the English ranks could be broken. It is said that twice during the afternoon William ordered his knights to turn away, as though in retreat. Each time some Englishmen were drawn forward only to be surrounded and massacred.

Gaps now appeared in the wall of English shields. Late in the day the Normans finally broke through and Harold himself was killed. Looking at the Bayeux tapestry, it might seem that an arrow pierced his eye. But the man tugging at the arrow is one of the King's housecarls. Harold is next to him, being hacked down by a Norman knight.

King Harold's reign of forty weeks was over, and so was one of the most important battles in the history of Europe. As darkness fell the remains of the English army fled. They had fought with great courage, but in the end the better equipped and more disciplined side had won.

From Duke to King

The throne was vacant and within William's reach. But the Duke was not yet master of England. The powerful northern earls, Edwin and Morcar, had not fought in the great battle. William did not know whether they would try to stop him from being king. And he was not sure whether the people of London would resist him.

Norman cavalry charging some of Harold's *housecarls*, who put up a shield wall. Both sides are throwing spears

William did not march directly to London. He took a roundabout route, forcing the surrender of some important towns on the way. At Canterbury the Duke fell ill, and his advance was halted for a month. The English might have taken this opportunity to raise a fresh army, but they seemed afraid of William and unable to agree on a new leader. The only serious resistance to the Conqueror came when he reached London Bridge. Rather than try to take the narrow wooden bridge by force, William decided to encircle London and approach it from the north.

The Normans crossed the Thames at Wallingford, where there was a shallow ford and bridge. By the time they reached Berkhamsted the Londoners had decided to surrender. A party of leading Englishmen, including Edwin, Morcar and the rulers of the Church, met William and agreed to accept him as King. To make sure no one changed their minds, he ordered his soldiers to burn and destroy the surrounding countryside along the way from Berkhamsted to London.

On Christmas Day 1066 the Duke was crowned King William I at Westminster Abbey. Like the rulers before him he swore to govern justly. Although he had gained the crown by force he did not want his new subjects to think of him as a foreign conqueror. He claimed to be the rightful king—the first choice of Edward the Confessor. And he announced that Edward's laws must still be kept.

During the coronation ceremony all the people assembled in the church were asked to say whether they accepted William as their lord. A great shout of agreement went up. On hearing this, the Norman guards outside feared William was being attacked. They panicked and set fire to the buildings around the abbey. Amid the crackle of flames, the screams and the sound of brawling outside, William stayed calmly at the altar while the Archbishop of York finished the service. No one could doubt the new king's courage and determination!

King Harold drops his axe as he is struck down by a Norman knight. Above, we see the Latin words *Harold Rex Interfectus Est* (King Harold is killed)

Timeline—The Norman Conquest

A.D.

1042–66	Reign of Edward 'the Confessor'
1051	Duke William's visit to King Edward
probably 1064	Harold's oath to William
1066	6 January — Harold crowned King
	April — Halley's Comet
	25 September — Battle of Stamford Bridge
	14 October — Battle of Hastings
	25 December—William crowned King

More about the Norman Conquest

Books

M. E. Reeves, *The Norman Conquest* (Longman, Then and There series). Pages 1–25.

1066 (Cape, History Jackdaw series, No. 38). Contains a collection of contemporary documents, edited for use in schools.

D. Scott-Daniell, *Battles and Battlefields* (Batsford). Chapters 1 and 2 for Stamford Bridge and Hastings.

N. Denny and J. Filmer-Sankey, *The Bayeux Tapestry* (Collins).

A. F. Titterton, *The Bayeux Tapestry* (Ginn's History Bookshelves, Green Shelf).

Filmstrips

The Bayeux Tapestry (B.B.C. *Radiovision*, B.B.C. Publications).

The Bayeux Tapestry, Parts 1 and 2 (Visual Publications).

The Norman Conquest (Visual Information Service).

Ciné Film

The Bayeux Tapestry (Films de Compas, distributed by Educational Foundation for Visual Aids).

Visit

An exact copy of the Bayeux Tapestry in the Victoria and Albert Museum, London. Other reproductions can be found in the Art Galleries at Reading and Nottingham.

To write

1 Imagine there is a *south* wind throughout August 1066. So William lands then and Hardrada does not arrive until the end of September. Tell the story of what *might* have happened—how the weather could have changed the course of history!

2 To what extent was Edward the Confessor responsible for the troubles of 1066?

3 *(a)* Make a list of all the different races that settled in England from Roman times to the eleventh century.
(b) Draw a map of western Europe with arrows to show where each wave of invaders came from.

10   The Rule of the Conqueror

King William's first task was to reward the Norman and French barons who had fought for him. He gave them lands taken from English thanes who had died in battle or fled overseas.

English nobles who swore to serve William were allowed to keep their lands. But they had no real power. The King put his trust in Norman lords—men such as Bishop Odo, his half-brother, who became Earl of Kent, and his cousin William FitzOsbern, Earl of Hereford. The chief English earls were kept in the royal court much of the time, under the watchful eye of the King. They grew more and more discontented, and it was not long before leading Englishmen rose in open rebellion against their foreign masters.

William I, as shown on one of his coins

'The harrying of the North'

William spent most of 1067 in Normandy, where he still ruled as Duke. While he was away an armed rising had to be put down in Kent. And when he returned to England the King had to march down to Exeter and force its citizens to obey him. More risings followed, and William moved about the country building castles for defence against his new subjects.

The greatest threat to the Normans came in 1069, when there was a rebellion in the North. One of the King's foreign earls was killed in a quarrel and thousands of Englishmen took up arms. Fuel was added to the flames when a fleet of 200 Danish ships appeared off the east coast. They sailed up the Humber and joined the rebels. York was ransacked and the Normans driven out. The King and his barons were outnumbered and in serious danger. But William kept his nerve and took full advantage of the lack of leadership on the other side. He marched north, stamping out opposition as he went. The Danes took to their boats and York was soon recaptured.

William had dealt mercifully with earlier risings, but this time he got really tough. To prevent any chance of further trouble he led his men through Yorkshire and deliberately destroyed the country-side. Every village was burnt to the ground. Cattle, sheep and pigs were slaughtered, and stores of food set on fire. It was mid-winter, so thousands of peasants died of cold and hunger.

The Conqueror had no more trouble from the northern English, but it was a terrible revenge. 'Never before did William commit so much cruelty', wrote a Norman monk, 'I dare not praise him for a deed which brought ruin to all, good and bad.' For nearly a century the lands that William *harried* (destroyed, or laid waste) were like a desert.

William still faced one last rebel stronghold, in the *Fens* of East Anglia—a wide area of flat, marshy land full of swamps and streams. On one of the 'islands' of dry land, at Ely, a brave band of English rebels had gathered. They were led by a Lincolnshire thane called Hereward, nicknamed 'the Wake' because he was wide awake and watchful. He was famous for his great strength and his skill as a swordsman.

In the summer of 1071 William set out to conquer the Fens. It was easier said than done. He had to use boats to get his army across the marshes. And even then he could find no way of reaching the rebels until monks from Ely Abbey showed his soldiers a secret pathway. Most of the English were finally rounded up and killed, although Hereward himself probably escaped. Many stories are told about his adventures, but we do not know for certain what happened to him.

Thus it took William five years of hard fighting before he could really call himself master of England. The rebellions finally convinced him that he could not trust the English leaders. After 1069 he took most of the lands still held by Englishmen and gave them to Normans. Nearly all royal officials and the leading members of his household were foreigners. Gradually even the Church came to be ruled by bishops and abbots from the Continent.

Norman castles

William's barons were hated foreigners on English soil. They could not risk living in undefended halls or houses. Instead they built castles, and shut themselves inside whenever danger threatened.

There was no time to lose, so the earliest castles were built of wood, which is quicker and easier to use than stone. If possible they were sited on a hill or cliff, to make them more difficult to attack. But if the ground was flat a great mound of earth called a *motte* was made, leaving a deep ditch all round. On top of the motte a stockade (wall of wooden stakes) was built and, inside this, a wooden tower or *keep.*

Artist's impression of a motte and bailey castle. Such wooden buildings perished long ago, but mounds and ditches of these castles can still be seen in many parts of England and France

A *mangonel*—a kind of catapult or stone-throwing machine

Beside the motte there was a kind of yard or enclosure called a *bailey.* This too was surrounded by a stockade, bank and ditch. Inside were living quarters, kitchens, storage huts, stables and work-shops. (The keep was normally occupied only when the castle was under attack.) All the back-breaking work of digging, cutting and carrying timber, and putting up the buildings was done by English peasants.

No baron could build a castle for himself without the King's permission. William wanted to be sure that all castles were in the hands of trusted men who would not rebel against him. Some of his most loyal supporters were given the task of building royal castles and guarding them for the King. Royal castles were built in all the main towns, to keep the people in order and to provide safe places where county sheriffs could be based. If the best site for such a castle was already occupied by houses these were knocked down and families made homeless. In Lincoln, 166 houses were destroyed to make room for a royal castle!

Before long the Normans were busy strengthening their castles with stone walls round the motte and bailey. These were more difficult to break down than wooden stockades, and they could not be set on fire. The wooden keep on the motte usually remained. The result was a *shell-keep*—a wooden building inside protected by a hard outer ring or 'shell' of stone.

Despite this extra protection, attackers found ways of breaking into shell-keeps. If there was a *moat* (a water-filled ditch crossed only by a drawbridge) they built a crossing with stones, earth and wood. Then they brought up ladders and wooden *siege towers,* which were tall enough for men on top to shoot arrows over the wall. Sometimes the attackers tried to make a hole in the wall. Huge boulders were fired from machines like catapults, and battering-rams were used. These were iron-tipped tree-trunks, which swung on chains between posts.

In defence, the castle guards fired showers of arrows, dropped stones and tried to set fire to ladders, siege towers and other equip-ment. If the attackers failed to break into the castle they might camp nearby and try to starve out the defenders by cutting off supplies from outside. This could take a long time, because a castle usually had its own well for water and ample storage space for food and weapons.

By far the strongest Norman castles were *stone keeps* or 'great towers', usually square in shape. The first of these was the White Tower, built by William in London to guard the approach to the city up the Thames. Other buildings have been added since the Conqueror's day, making up what we call the Tower of London. The massive Norman keep still stands in the centre, ninety feet high with walls up to fifteen feet thick.

William also had stone keeps at Exeter and Colchester. But most castles of this type were built in the next century. The Conqueror's youngest son, Henry I, built several—including the one pictured, at Rochester. On the ground floor of a stone keep food and weapons were stored and prisoners locked in dungeons. The main entrance was usually above, on the first floor, reached by an outside flight of steps. This led into a great hall, the main room of the castle. Meals were eaten in the hall, and at night the castle guards slept there.

Stone keeps were dark, draughty places to live in. But they were built for safety rather than comfort. The windows were narrow slits, too small for attackers to squeeze through; and the entrance was protected by a *portcullis,* a strong spiked door which closed from above. The walls of stone keeps were too high for siege towers and too thick for catapults or battering-rams. The most likely way of capturing such castles was to starve out the guards.

Kings, barons and knights

William's barons were not given their lands for nothing. In return they had to serve the King and provide him with mounted knights whenever he needed them. Before 1066, English thanes had also been expected to raise an army for their king. But the bargain they made with him was a rough and ready one. William made more definite arrangements. He demanded an exact number of knights from each of his nobles, depending on the size and value of their lands. The need to give military service in return for land is known as a *feudal system* (the Latin word *feudum* means land).

In the first place all land belonged to the King. He kept about a quarter of it as royal estates, where he and members of the court spent much time hunting the fox, deer and wild boar. The rest of the kingdom was shared out among the nobles—earls, barons and bishops. These were the *tenants-in-chief,* holding land directly from the Crown.

Before a tenant-in-chief received his estates he went through a ceremony of *homage.* He knelt, placed his hands between the King's, and said: 'I promise to become your man, to hold these lands faithfully and perform my due service.' Then the King told his tenant what was expected of him. He must always be ready to fight for the King, and bring along a certain number of knights. It might be a dozen or as many as fifty. Occasionally he would have to provide 'castle-guard' (knights to defend a royal castle). Bishops and abbots

A Norman knight. He is protected by chain-mail, made of small metal rings sewn on to a backing of leather or strong linen

How the land was held
(Simplified diagram of 'Feudal Duties')

LAND held in return　　　　　　　　　　　　　　　*for SERVICES*

King
(The 'Feudal Lord' or
owner of the kingdom)

The King keeps some
royal estates and
distributes the rest
among his
tenants-in-chief.

Tenants-in-chief,
mainly through the
services of their
under-tenants,
support the King.

Tenants-in-chief
(Barons, Bishops, etc.)
About 200 – 300

Tenants-in-chief
keep some estates, or
manors, and distribute
the rest among
their under-tenants.

Under-tenants,
by their service
(usually in war),
support
tenants-in-chief.

Under-tenants
(Knights, etc)
a few thousand

Under-tenants keep
some land, or *demesne*,
and divide the rest
among their peasants.

Peasants, by their labour,
support under-tenants.

Peasants
(Village labourers)
1 – 1½ million

The White Tower—the keep of the Tower of London. It was built by the Normans between 1078 and 1090, on the site of an earlier wooden castle put up as soon as William arrived in London

had to provide knights, just as barons did, but they were not expected to go to war themselves.

Some barons kept their knights close at hand, living in their castle. Then they were ready to fight at short notice. This was often necessary in troubled areas such as the Welsh borderlands, where there was always the danger of a surprise attack. But usually a tenant-in-chief divided up some of the lands the King had granted him and gave his knights small estates, or *manors,* of their own. A manor normally contained at least one village. These knights thus became *under-tenants* and were able to support themselves.

An under-tenant swore homage to his lord, just as the lord had done to the King. William saw the danger in this. In France and Germany, tenants-in-chief sometimes got their knights to fight for them *against* the king. So William made it clear that all under-tenants must be faithful to the King first, before any other man.

The King's fighting strength depended on a good supply of trained knights. A boy began his preparation for knighthood at about the age of seven, serving as a page in a lord's household and learning how gentlemen should behave. Later, at about fifteen, he became a knight's *squire,* or personal servant. He was always at his master's side, and learned to ride, wear armour and use weapons so that he could go with him into battle. At about twenty he was ready to be a knight himself. Sometimes younger squires showed great bravery in war and were knighted there and then. But normally a special ceremony was performed. The squire spent all night praying at an altar and confessed his sins. Then, in front of his lord, a sword and spurs were fastened on and he swore to be loyal, brave and well-mannered.

How did the coming of the Normans affect ordinary peasants? After 1066 there were fewer *freeholders*—men who rented land without having to give services in return. But the lives of most country folk hardly changed. Instead of serving an English thane, peasants served a French-speaking lord of the manor (see Chapter 11). This lord might be a knight or a baron (the land a tenant-in-chief kept for himself was also divided into manors). Not until the thirteenth and fourteenth centuries were peasants expected to do military service in any large numbers. By then there was a need for larger armies, containing many ordinary footsoldiers.

The stone keep built by Henry I at Rochester in Kent. Notice how it dominates the crossing of the river Medway. It is 113 feet high and has four floors inside (one more than the White Tower in London)

Domesday Book

At Christmas 1085 William called his usual Great Council of barons and bishops. The *Anglo-Saxon Chronicle,* still kept going by the monks of Peterborough, tells us that '. . . the King had much thought and very deep speech with his Council about this land—how it was peopled and with what sort of men'. In future, instead of guessing he wanted to know exactly how much land each tenant held, what taxes he could expect, and so on. He ordered that a detailed survey of England should be made without delay.

Royal officials were sent round the kingdom, and in each village they asked a long list of questions. They wanted to know who was the lord and who had owned the land before the Conquest; what it was worth and how much of it was ploughland, meadow, pasture and woodland. They also wrote down the number of freeholders, *villeins* (ordinary peasants) and *bordars* (poorer peasants). Even water-mills, fishponds and livestock were counted.

So thorough was the survey that it was said there was not an ox, cow or pig left out! Here is part of the account of Birmingham, then a tiny village:

Richard holds Bermingeham of William (William FitzAnsculf, a tenant-in-chief) . . . There is land for 6 ploughs; there is one plough in the *demesne* (Richard's private land). There are 5 villeins and 4 bordars and 2 ploughs. There is a wood half a mile long and 4 furlongs broad. In the time of King Edward it was worth 20 shillings, and it is still worth the same.

The survey was finished before the end of 1086, and hundreds of parchment rolls were taken to the King. He did not study them long as he was about to leave for Normandy. At Winchester, royal clerks arranged the information under counties and finally made up two great volumes which came to be called *Domesday Book*. Domesday means the Day of Judgment. The book got this name because the facts in it could not be ignored or avoided by anyone, just like the Judgment Day.

Accounts of a few towns, including London, have not been found. Nevertheless, for the first time we can work out England's total population fairly accurately. It was about $1\frac{1}{2}$ million in 1086—roughly equal to the combined populations of Liverpool and Manchester today. Domesday Book also shows the full effects of the Norman Conquest. County by county a new ruling class of foreigners had replaced the English thanes who once served Edward the Confessor.

'Stronger than any king before'

William never saw Domesday Book in its finished form. He met his death in the summer of 1087, while fighting the King of France. He was riding through the French town of Nantes, which his army had set on fire, when his horse trod on a smouldering piece of wood. It shied and threw the sixty-year old King heavily against the iron *pommel* (knob) on the front of his saddle. William was seriously injured and died a month later (9 September).

The two large volumes which make up Domesday Book. They are kept in the Public Record Office, London. Thanks to this great survey we know more about England under the Normans than in any earlier period

Many Englishmen remembered him as a hard, cruel king. He had humbled the English thanes, harried the North, demanded heavy taxes and made harsh forest laws to protect his animals from poachers. Any man who killed a deer had his eyes put out. Hunting was William's greatest joy, and he increased the size of the royal forests. In Hampshire over sixty villages were destroyed and hundreds of families made homeless when a large area of woodland and rough pasture was taken over for the King's sport. Today it is still called the New Forest.

Certainly William was a man to be feared. But he was also respected for his courage, hard work and skill as a king. Many chroniclers praised him. An Englishman who had lived in his household wrote:

King William was . . . stronger than any king before. He was gentle to the good men who loved God, and stern beyond all measure to those who disobeyed him . . . Amongst other things the good peace he made in this land is not to be forgotten—so that any honest man could travel over his kingdom unharmed with his pockets full of gold.'

The Conqueror divided his lands and wealth between his three sons. Henry, the youngest, got £5,000 in silver. Robert, the eldest, became duke of Normandy. The English crown went to William, the second son and his father's favourite. William II was short, fat and red-faced, which explains his nickname 'Rufus' (Latin for red). When he got angry or excited he stuttered so badly that no one could understand him. Rufus was harsh and unpopular but, like his father, he was a strong king. His subjects were afraid to disobey him.

In August 1100, Rufus was mysteriously killed by an arrow while hunting in the New Forest. His companions said it was an accident, but it could well have been murder. Almost as though he had planned it, William's brother Henry seized the royal treasure at Winchester and rode to London, where he was crowned only three days after Rufus's death. As a man, Henry I was cruel and greedy. But he was a firm and wise ruler. For thirty-five years he gave England order and justice.

In the powerful grip of the Conqueror and his sons England went through many changes. The close link with Normandy resulted in more trade and travel across the Channel. New ideas were introduced from Europe, including fighting on horseback. And a new language—Norman French—was brought to England by William and his followers. In time many French words crept into the English still spoken by ordinary peasants.

Under bishops and abbots from the Continent the English Church became stricter. Monks kept more closely to their vows, and priests were better educated. Within a century the Normans rebuilt many parish churches and most of the country's cathedrals and abbeys. Numerous old churches in England still have traces of Norman stonework: rounded arches, round-headed windows, thick walls and huge pillars. Such buildings were massive and very strong—like the Normans themselves.

Extract from an illustrated manuscript; showing King Henry I at sea

Part of the interior of
Gloucester Cathedral,
showing rounded Norman
arches and massive pillars

More about Norman England

Some later developments in castle building are described in Chapter 16.

Books

M. E. Reeves, *The Norman Conquest* (Longman, Then and There series). Pages 26–51.

D. Birt and J. Nichol, *The Norman Conquest* (Longman History Games).

H. Loyn and A. Sorrell, *Norman Britain* (Lutterworth).

R. E. Latham, *Finding Out About the Normans* (Muller).

M. E. Reeves, *The Medieval Castle* (Longman, Then and There series).

A. F. Titterton, *English Castles* (Ginn's History Bookshelves, Green Shelf).

R. Arnold, *Kings, Bishops, Knights and Pawns* (Longman Young Books). Describes 'feudal' society in England and abroad.

Domesday Book (Cape, History Jackdaw series, no. 39).

D. Grinnell-Milne, *The Killing of William Rufus* (David and Charles Books).

The Norman Realm (Longman, History Project Kits). For reference.

Hereward the Wake, a novel by Charles Kingsley.

W. K. Ritchie, *Scotland and the Normans* (Longman, Then and There series).

Filmstrips

The Medieval World (Longman, Then and There Filmstrips). No. 1 for knights and castles.

The Castle (Common Ground, Medieval Life).

Let's Visit Britain's Castles (Daily Mail, distributed by Educational Foundation for Visual Aids).

The Domesday Book (Educational Audio Visual Ltd.).

Ciné Film

The Medieval Castle (Gaumont British Film Library).

Visit

The nearest castle, or ruins of one. Try to find out:

when it was built.

whether it was a royal or baronial castle.

whether anyone famous ever lived there.

why the particular site was chosen.

how it was defended and the best ways of attacking it.

whether it was ever besieged and/or captured.

To write

1 Look again at the last section of Chapter 8. Then compare the ways William and Cnut treated the conquered English. Would you have acted differently in either case?

2 Make a 'Glossary of Feudalism', including the meanings of such terms as tenant-in-chief, under-tenant, villein, homage, manor, page, squire and demesne.

3 Imagine you are a baron who has decided to build a castle in your town or village. Suggest *three* suitable sites, and explain why you think each is a good defensive position.

11 Life on an English Manor

Imagine we are flying low over England in an aeroplane when suddenly, below us, the clock is turned back seven or eight hundred years. How would the landscape differ from that of the twentieth century? Of course we would no longer see railways, motor traffic, electricity pylons or great industrial towns. But the thing that would strike us most of all would be the strange wildness of the countryside.

Nowhere would we see the familiar 'patchwork quilt' of neatly enclosed fields—the main feature of the landscape today. Instead, great areas of forest, moor and marshland would stretch out before us, hardly touched by the hand of man. We would only see farming land as we approached the scattered villages and towns. Even then we would notice a marked difference from present-day agriculture. In the Middle Ages crops were usually cultivated in *open* fields, without hedges or walls.

The villages below us would be smaller than they are now, having perhaps twenty or thirty dwellings clustered round a stone church. Probably the only other stone building in the village would be the lord's manor house. At this time villages were either manors or parts of manors, controlled by one of the king's feudal lords.

In this chapter we will take a closer look at village life during the two or three centuries following the Norman conquest. Conditions were much the same in many parts of Europe. So from studying England we can get a good idea of the way millions of other people lived.

Below: aerial view of part of Laxton in Nottinghamshire, where the medieval 'open field' system of agriculture is still carried on *Right:* in contrast, a modern 'patchwork quilt' of enclosed fields

Peasants and their homes

The Normans called most ordinary peasants *villeins* (from the French word *ville,* meaning a village or town). A villein was not free. He was 'tied to the soil'; forbidden to leave the manor without the lord's permission. His land, his home, even the villein himself was the property of the lord.

Villeins lived in small one- or two-roomed huts. These usually had a main framework of timber, filled in with *wattle and daub*—plaited twigs smeared with mud. Roofs were thatched with straw or reeds. Inside, the floor was simply hard-trodden earth, perhaps spread with rushes gathered from beside the village stream. Windows had no glass; they were covered with wooden shutters. This meant huts were very dark in cold weather, when shutters had to be closed.

In the middle of the floor a wood fire burned on a stone slab. There was no chimney, so the smoke escaped as best it could. The inside of the hut was therefore very sooty. It was smelly too, because dogs, pigs and chickens shared the living space with the family!

All furniture was home-made: a few stools, a trestle table, which could be folded away after use, and a wooden chest for clothes. Beds were just bags of straw, covered with rough woollen blankets. An iron cauldron was used for cooking. On the walls of the hut hung a spade, hoe, rake and other tools. Dangling from the rafters would be bunches of dried herbs, onions and perhaps a side of bacon. Other food was kept in baskets.

Meals were very plain and varied little from day to day. Breakfast, at dawn, was no more than a lump of dry bread and a mug of watery ale. At ten or eleven in the morning men returned from the fields for dinner. Lumps of bread and cheese, perhaps flavoured with an onion, were washed down with ale or cider. There might be a little fish or salted meat too.

When the day's work was over, usually at about five o'clock, it was

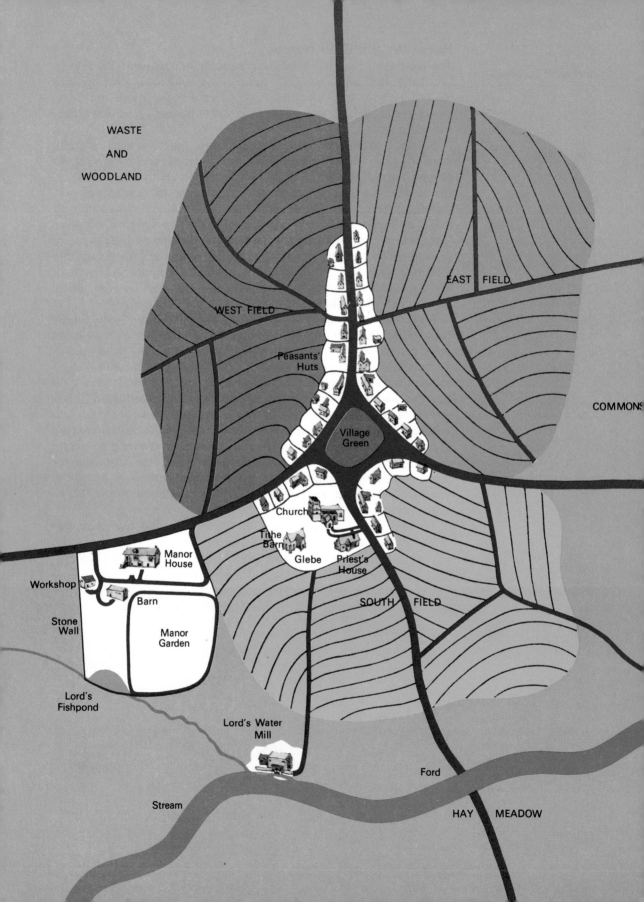

WASTE

AND

WOODLAND

EAST FIELD

WEST FIELD

COMMONS

Peasants'
Huts

Village
Green

Church

Tithe
Barn

Glebe

Priest's
House

Manor
House

Workshop

Barn

SOUTH   FIELD

Stone
Wall

Manor
Garden

Lord's
Fishpond

Lord's Water
Mill

Ford

Stream

HAY   MEADOW

Left: Plan of an 'open field' village. Strips were usually marked out with lines of wooden pegs or stones. The size of the three fields was not fixed; as the village population grew, more land was brought into cultivation. There was no proper roads, only rough tracks or paths

time for supper. This began with hot *pottage* (a thick vegetable soup) which was followed by bread, cheese, fresh fruit in summer and the usual ale or cider. After each meal the wooden plates were scraped with a knife and wiped with grass.

During the summer months country folk spent most of their time out-of-doors. But in cold weather they sat at home doing useful jobs. Men repaired tools, made boots from cow-hide, and furniture, plates and cups from wood. Women spun and wove wool into coarse cloth, plaited reeds into baskets, and made rushlights from peeled rushes soaked in animal fat. These gave a feeble light, so peasant families went to bed early.

Almost everything villeins needed had to be made at home, or by one of the village tradesmen. Every manor had its blacksmith, carpenter and others with special jobs to do. The only essential goods brought in from outside were salt and iron. Otherwise each village was self-supporting. Few peasants ever travelled more than a few miles, to the nearest market town. Their knowledge of the outside world was based on gossip and stories told by passing travellers. With no sense of distance, London must have seemed as far off to them as Rome or Jerusalem!

'Open field' farming

The Normans brought no new methods of agriculture to England. Peasants carried on farming the land as their forefathers had done for centuries. Over a large part of the country, especially in the Midlands and the South, the village *arable-* or plough-land was cultivated in three large open fields. These were divided into narrow plots, or strips, which were shared out among the villagers. Each man's strips were scattered about all three fields, so good and bad soil was evenly distributed.

Each villager looked after his own strips. But for some jobs, including ploughing, he joined forces with his neighbours. Few peasants owned enough oxen (bullocks) to pull a heavy plough. So groups of villagers worked together, each contributing a share in the ploughing team. Eight oxen might be needed altogether, although teams of four or even two could be used on light soils.

Below: Peasants ploughing. The plough was mostly made of wood, but its cutting parts (the *coulter* and *share*) were made of iron. The large part by the ploughman's foot is the *mould-board.* It pushes the soil sideways and helps to make the furrow. A plough team was difficult to turn, so long strips were better than square plots

When the land was ploughed corn crops were sown—perhaps wheat or rye in one field in the autumn, and barley in another in the spring. The third field remained *fallow* (unsown after ploughing) so that the soil could recover its richness. The fallow period came to each field in rotation, one year out of three. There were no artificial fertilisers in the Middle Ages. If corn was sown on the same land every year the soil got poorer and poorer.

As well as his strips each villein had a small patch of land round his hut. Here he grew peas, beans, leeks, onions and other vegetables. Perhaps he had fruit trees too, providing apples, pears or cherries in season. Some of the poorest peasants, called *bordars* or *cottars*, had no strips in the fields and thus depended on their 'cottage gardens'. However, the lord usually hired them for money when extra hands were needed.

Beyond the open fields there were areas of rough pasture and wasteland. These were the *commons*, where villagers grazed their cattle and sheep during the warmer months. Pigs were taken into the nearby woods in the autumn to be fattened on acorns and beech nuts. In the woods peasants also gathered wild fruits, berries and logs for fuel.

Each villein also had a share in the meadow, which lay beside the river, where grass grew longest. In June or July the meadow-grass was cut to make hay for the animals' winter fodder. There was never enough hay to keep all the animals alive until the spring. So the older ones were killed off in the autumn and the flesh salted to preserve it. Such meat must have been very tough to eat.

Between the hay-making and cattle-slaughtering came the busiest time of the year—the corn harvest in August. Men toiled from dawn until dusk in the great fields, and women and children gave a helping hand. If the harvest was poor or spoilt by heavy rain the villagers might face starvation before the winter was out. Sometimes there were

Left: Sowing the crops. The peasants normally had seeds in baskets or bags. They broadcast (scattered) them by hand into the furrows

Above: Cutting hay with a long curved scythe. Dry weather was essential, otherwise the hay might be spoilt. Hence the saying 'make hay while the sun shines'

Above: Harvesting the corn with a sickle. This is smaller than a scythe and has a crescent-shaped blade. When the corn was cut it was tied into sheaves and taken to the barns

Right: Threshing (beating) the corn, to get the grains out of their husks. It was done with jointed sticks called flails. Sacks of grain were then taken to the miller to be ground into flour

terrible famines, when thousands of peasants were reduced to eating dogs and rotting garbage.

The hilly areas of the North and West were not suited to 'open field' farming. Here people lived mainly off sheep, goats and cattle. They had no need to work together on the land, so they lived in smaller groups or even in isolated dwellings.

Duties to the lord

Very few, if any, of the villagers were freeholders, who simply rented land and were free to come and go as they wished. All the ordinary peasants, the villeins, had to work for the lord of the manor.

The lord had land of his own, called the *demesne* (pronounced demain). It included strips in the open fields, which the villeins had to cultivate. Normally this took them two or three half-days each week. But during hay-making, harvesting and other busy periods they did extra or *boon* work. The lord provided free meals at boon times. Nevertheless villeins hated these extra duties because their own work was delayed.

To make sure the peasants did their duties properly, the lord appointed a foreman called a *reeve*. He was usually an ordinary villein, just as a school prefect is one of the pupils. The reeve had to know the farming customs of the manor and see the necessary tools were ready for each task. He even checked that the villeins began work on time. In return the lord paid him a small wage.

If a lord had several manors he could not supervise them all personally. He put each in charge of a *bailiff*, or manager, who looked after his affairs while he was absent. Bailiffs were free-men, not villeins, and they needed some education because they kept the accounts of the manor.

As well as working on the demesne, villeins had to give the lord some of their produce—perhaps a dozen eggs at Easter, some corn in

the autumn and a hen at Christmastide. Villeins had no choice but to grind their corn in the lord's mill and bake their bread in his ovens. Then the lord took a proportion of each man's flour and bread as payment for his services!

A villein could not sell his livestock at market, nor give his daughter in marriage, without getting the lord's permission and paying him. Similarly, when a villein died his son paid for the right to take over his land. Such matters were settled in regular meetings of the manor court, headed by the lord or his chief official, the *steward*.

The manor court also dealt with wrongdoers who broke the customs of the manor. For example, a villein might have been caught grinding corn with a hand-mill instead of paying to use the lord's mill. If the freeholders or other responsible villagers declared him guilty he paid a fine in money or goods. Villeins were often tempted to steal. Huts had no locks on the doors, and the lord's orchard, fishpond and hunting grounds were very inviting. Indeed, the word villein (now spelt villain) has come to mean a rogue or wrongdoer.

Not surprisingly some villeins tried to avoid the duties of the manor by running away to the nearest town. If an escaped villein was not captured within a year and a day he was free. But his life would still be hard. Towns had few jobs for men with no skills other than farming. In time, more and more peasants saved up and *bought* their freedom by paying the lord a lump sum and a yearly rent for their land.

A bailiff directing operations at harvest time

The lord's manor house

Some great lords lived in castles. But on most manors the lord's home was a stone house, perhaps surrounded by a high wall or moat. Like castles, manor houses often had cellars on the ground floor and the main room, or hall, on the first floor. In the hall meals were served, and at other times women of the household did their spinning and em-

100

broidery, children played, and the lord gave orders to his servants. The manor court was often held in the hall, and every night most of the servants slept there, on benches or on the rushes covering the oak floor.

Early manor houses had a fireplace in the middle of the hall. The smoke escaped through an opening in the roof. In later years a brick fireplace and chimney was built into one of the walls. But even with a roaring fire the hall was cold and draughty in winter. One way of checking draughts was to hang tapestries on the walls. Another way was to build a wooden screen just inside the main entrance to the hall. Doors were cut in the screen and often a minstrels' gallery was built above it.

Next to the hall was a private room called the *bower*, where guests were received. Here the lord, his lady and their younger children also slept. The lord's bed had curtains round it to keep out draughts. Clothes were kept in heavy wooden chests, but there were no upholstered chairs and carpets were rare. The kitchen was well away from the living quarters, because of the fire-risk. Next to it was the

A water mill. The wheel turns two great grindstones inside, and these grind the grains of corn into flour. Some villages had a windmill instead, but these were uncommon. In fact windmills were unknown in England before the late twelfth century

pantry, large enough to hold whole carcasses of meat, and a *buttery* ('bottlery') where wine and ale were stored.

Fruit trees, vegetables and flowers grew in the garden. The lady of the manor also planted herbs, which she used to make medicines for the sick people of the village. Nearby, there was a fishpond and various farm buildings, including a barn, cattle-shed and stables. As time went by manor houses were enlarged, with extra bedrooms, cellars and a chapel. If the lord was very wealthy he might have glass windows put in. But glass was a great extravagance, normally used only in large churches and the richest homes.

The remains of Stokesay 'Castle'—a manor house in Shropshire. Notice the stone keep, built in case of attack. This really makes it a cross between a castle and a house

Eating in the hall

The lord and his household usually got up at dawn. After a breakfast of bread, meat and ale, both lord and lady were kept busy giving instructions to the servants. Then, if the weather was fine, the lord and his bailiff might ride round the manor, to see that all was in order. His children, meanwhile, had lessons in Latin and French, sometimes from the village parson.

Everyone was hungry and ready for dinner before midday. The lord and older members of his family sat at the 'high table'. This stood across the end of the hall, on a low platform, or *dais*. Servants, young children and others of lower rank sat on benches at trestle tables, put up lengthwise down the hall. At each place the butler laid spoons, knives, drinking cups and bread rolls. Salt cellars were also put out.

There were no table forks. Most eating was done with the fingers, so pages carried round jugs of water and napkins. After a bowl of vegetable soup the main course was served. It might consist of boiled beef or mutton, roast pork, or perhaps bream or roach, boiled in ale and salt water. Fish was always eaten on Fridays, as ruled by the Church. The meal ended with cheese and sometimes a sweet, such as fruit tart, pancakes or egg custard. Ale was the usual drink.

Thd second main meal was supper, at about five o'clock. The food was similar to that eaten for dinner; unless the lord had important guests at his table, when a big feast would be held. Then silver goblets were placed on the high table and French wine was served. Venison or a whole pig might be roasted, or perhaps poultry was served—pheasant, goose, duck or even peacock.

When darkness fell the hall was lit by tall wax candles or flaming torches stuck in iron holders round the walls. A travelling acrobat or jester might be hired to entertain the guests, while in the gallery minstrels sang and played long stories in verse, called ballads. After a time the ladies retired to the bower, leaving the men to their drinking and talking. Under the tables dogs eagerly snapped up bones thrown down for them.

Pastimes and festivals

The lord spent much time hunting in the woods and scrubland. If there were no deer or wild boar on his manor, badgers and hares were tracked down with a pack of mastiffs, wolf-hounds and terriers. Hawking was another favourite pastime. The lord's falconer trained hawks to perch on the wrist with hoods over their heads. At the sight of a wild duck, heron, crane or other suitable prey the hood was removed and the hawk allowed to fly.

When their lessons were over the lord's children enjoyed games that are still popular today. They had hoops, tops and skipping ropes.

A Norman manor house at Boothby Pagnell in Lincolnshire. Notice the steps leading up to the first floor, and the rounded arches over the door and most of the windows. The chimney was put in later. So was the large square window. Early manor houses were dark inside because, without glass, windows had to be very small (to reduce draughts)

On a squared board they played draughts, backgammon and chess. Boys loved to go horse-riding and practice shooting with bows and arrows. Their sisters were taught embroidery, singing and dancing. Many girls were married in their early teens, so they had a brief childhood. 'Love matches' were rare in well-to-do families. Most marriages were arranged by the parents when the future bride and bridegroom were children.

Peasant children had little time for play, because they had to help their parents. They fetched water from the well or stream, looked after the family's animals and did odd jobs around the hut. However, on Sundays and summer evenings they played tag, blind man's buff and made swings or see-saws. Their parents enjoyed dancing on the village green and other simple pleasures. Occasionally there were family celebrations, which gave some peasants a welcome break from their daily toil. After a wedding, 'bride ales' were drunk, and often funerals were an excuse for heavy drinking. Some villages had an ale-house where such gatherings were held.

Throughout the year there were regular village festivals. Spring was a special time for rejoicing, after the long, dark winter. On 1 May two young folk were chosen as King and Queen of the May and crowned with garlands of flowers. Then everyone danced round a maypole. On Midsummer Night, in June, the villagers had a feast round a big bonfire. A greasy pole might be set up with a leg of mutton on top for the first man to climb it. Later on, when the hay-cutting was finished, some lords released a sheep into the meadow. The peasants caught it and roasted it whole.

Other festivals were held on Church *holy days*—this is how we get the word 'holiday'. Each Sunday was a holy day of rest, when everyone went to mass. And there were about fifty more holy days in the calendar. Not all were kept, but on most manors there were fifteen to twenty holidays every year, at great religious festivals such as Christmas, Easter and Whit.

A lord's high table. Instead of plates, slices of stale bread called *trenchers* were put out. These were collected up after the meal and given to the poor. Today, when a wealthy man gives away something he has no use for we speak of 'crumbs from the rich man's table'

Before Christmas peasants gathered 'Yule logs' from the woods, and holly, ivy and mistletoe to decorate their huts. Most lords gave a Christmas feast for everyone, in the manor house. In February came the start of Lent, a time of fasting which went on until Easter. On Shrove Tuesday, the day before the Lenten fast, any remaining eggs were used up to make pancakes. When Easter Sunday arrived children were given gaily painted eggs and the church was decorated with spring flowers.

More about medieval villages

Books

M. E. Reeves, *The Medieval Village* (Longman, Then and There series).

A. F. Titterton, *Work on a Manor* and *Life in a Manor House* (Ginn's History Bookshelves, Green Shelf).

P. Andrewes, *A Thirteenth Century Villein* (O.U.P., People of the Past).

J. West, *The Medieval Forest* (Longman, Then and There series).

The queen from a chess set used in the Middle Ages. It was probably made of walrus-tusk, in Scotland

Filmstrips

The Medieval World (Longman, Then and There Filmstrips). No. 2: Country life, sports and pastimes.

The Village (Common Ground, Medieval Life).

The Three Field System—an 8mm. cassette film (Gateway).

Medieval Sports and Pastimes and The Medieval Manor (Educational Productions Ltd.).

Ciné Films

The Medieval Village (Gaumont British Film Library). Based on Laxton.

Medieval England (Gateway Film Productions Ltd.).

Visits

The village of Laxton in Nottinghamshire (three miles off the A1 road near Tuxford) continues to use the medieval 'open field' system.

A medieval manor house. Examples include Boothby Pagnell (Lincs), Haddon Hall (Derbyshire), Compton Castle (Devon) and Stokesay Castle (Shropshire)—both fortified manor houses.

To write and find out

1 In what ways was a medieval manor house less comfortable than most modern houses?

2 From the description in this chapter draw or paint a picture of the inside of a peasant's hut.

3 *(a)* Why did the Church forbid the eating of meat on Fridays? Do Catholics still have this rule today?

(b) Neither the lord nor his villeins had drinks such as coffee, tea or cocoa. When was each of these introduced into Britain?

12 Henry II and Thomas Becket

One moonlit night in 1120 a fine vessel called *The White Ship* was crossing the Channel from Normandy to England. On board was Prince William, son of Henry I, along with many barons and ladies of noble birth. The sea was calm and the passengers in good spirits. But all of a sudden there was a crashing and jolting. The ship had struck a rock and a gaping hole was torn in its wooden hull. Only one man, a servant, lived to tell the tale.

The loss of *The White Ship* had tragic results for England. It meant Henry I had no son to rule after him. Before his death, in 1135, he named his daughter Matilda as the heir to the throne. But the idea of a woman ruler was not popular, and Matilda was proud and domineering. A large group of barons gave their support to Henry's nephew, Count Stephen, who was crowned king.

Matilda stood up for her rights and gathered an army to fight Stephen. The outcome was civil war, with all the powerful men in the kingdom taking sides. Some barons saw the chance to increase their wealth by robbery and murder. They built castles without the King's permission and rode about the countryside with their own private armies. Poor Stephen was so busy fighting his enemies that the government of England was neglected. Men openly broke the laws and escaped punishment. The peace and order established by the Conqueror and his sons was shattered.

Coin showing King Stephen (1135–54). He was brave and honourable, but he failed to stop the lawlessness in his kingdom. A chronicler described his reign as 'nineteen long winters'

The first of the Plantagenets

After years of misery and bloodshed the two sides made a bargain. It was agreed that Stephen should reign as long as he lived, but Matilda's son, Henry, would be the next king. Within a year Stephen was dead. Henry sailed from France and was crowned at Westminster in December 1154. He was twenty-one years old; stocky, broad-shouldered and slightly bow-legged from much horse-riding. He had watchful grey eyes and dark red hair, closely cropped.

Henry II was the first of a long line of 'Plantagenet' kings, so called because the yellow broom flower (*planta genesta*) was the badge of his father, Geoffrey of Anjou. By the standards of the twelfth century Henry was well educated. He could read and write, and it was said that he had some knowledge of every language spoken from France to Palestine. However, he only knew French and Latin well. Although he could read English he never learned to speak it properly.

Nothing seemed to tire Henry. He worked far into the night yet was often busy again soon after dawn. He loved hunting and would ride all day until he was sore and blistered from the saddle. Such great energy made him hard to live with. He was always travelling from one palace or castle to the next, and sometimes gave his servants just a few hours to pack all the valuables, clothes, food, bedding, weapons

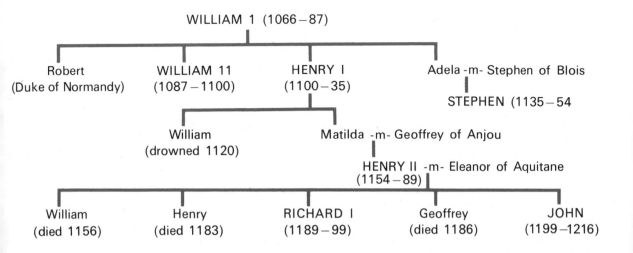

```
                        WILLIAM 1 (1066—87)

   Robert          WILLIAM 11        HENRY I          Adela -m- Stephen of Blois
(Duke of Normandy) (1087—1100)      (1100—35)
                                                         STEPHEN (1135—54

                William              Matilda -m- Geoffrey of Anjou
            (drowned 1120)
                                           HENRY II -m- Eleanor of Aquitane
                                             (1154—89)

  William          Henry          RICHARD I          Geoffrey           JOHN
(died 1156)      (died 1183)      (1189—99)        (died 1186)       (1199—1216)
```

Family tree of the Kings of England, 1066–1216

King Henry II's Empire. Henry was supposed to hold all his French lands as a tenant-in-chief of the King of France. He did his rightful homage to King Louis VII, but, like the Norman kings before, he was more powerful than his feudal overlord and never took orders from him!

and equipment of the entire court! Members of his household complained that he never sat down, except to eat. Even then he was busy reading a book, writing or discussing matters of government with his advisers.

Henry needed all his strength and energy, because he had vast possessions to govern. Besides England he ruled more than half of France. The northern French lands were inherited from his father and mother; except for Brittany, which he gained later. The lands in southern France, stretching down to the Spanish border, came to him as a result of his marriage, in 1152, to Eleanor, Countess of Aquitaine. Eleanor was more than ten years older than Henry. She was a lively, quick-witted woman, and must have greatly influenced the young King in the early part of his reign.

Henry restores order

England was again under a strong king, after nineteen years of law-lessness. Henry declared that every castle built in Stephen's reign must be destroyed. Within a year about 300 illegal castles were burned or pulled down. Meanwhile Henry sent home many foreign knights that had been hired by one side or the other during the civil war. And he set out to recover royal estates that Stephen had lost or given to greedy barons in return for their support.

Henry aimed to reduce the number of fighting men in the kingdom. Most wars took place on the Continent so there was no need to have thousands of knights at the ready in England. Many barons already preferred to make a payment called *scutage* (shield money) instead of giving the usual 'knight service', and Henry encouraged this. With the money collected he hired soldiers in France when he needed them.

Scutage soon became a kind of rent, paid regularly to the King in return for lands. This was sensible because it saved the cost of shipping a whole army across the Channel. But above all it meant that large numbers of knights gave up being professional soldiers and concentrated on looking after their manors. The country grew more peaceful, and troublesome barons were less of a threat to the King since they had fewer knights to call upon.

Henry chose many able and hardworking men as sheriffs, judges and ministers to help in the task of restoring law and order. Among them he had a special favourite—Thomas Becket, the son of a wealthy London merchant. Becket was living in the household of Theobald, Archbishop of Canterbury, when Henry came to the throne. Knowing Thomas to be intelligent and well-mannered, Theobald recommended him to the King who gave him the important position of Chancellor (royal chaplain and chief secretary).

Becket was fifteen years older than the King. Nevertheless the two men delighted in each other's company. 'When business was over for the day', wrote one of Becket's friends, 'the King and Thomas . . . used to play the fool together like a couple of boys.' They both loved sports and often went hawking and hunting.

Although he was a churchman, Becket lived in great luxury. His banquets were famous for their rich dishes and rare wines. He had six fully equipped ships to carry him between England and France, yet the King had only one! Henry knew his Chancellor outshone him but he did not mind. He was a generous-hearted man who cared little for fine living. As long as Thomas served him well he was satisfied.

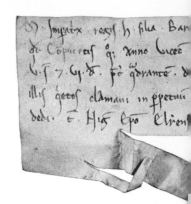

A royal *writ* (letter of command) from the twelfth century, sealed with the *Great Seal.* A lump of soft wax attached to the parchment was pressed in a hollow mould which had special designs cut on the inside. The result was a kind of signature, showing the document was genuine. As Chancellor, Becket had charge of the Great Seal. This meant all important documents passed through his hands

Late medieval woodcut showing a prisoner being tortured to confess his guilt

Royal justice

During Stephen's reign large numbers of men accused of crimes were tried by the barons in their own manor courts. Those found guilty paid heavy fines which went straight into the barons' pockets. Some nobles carried out the death penalty without royal permission and then seized the dead man's property. Henry was determined to put a stop to all this. In future he wanted serious offences to be tried only in the King's courts. Then people would have more chance of a fair trial and the money paid in fines would go into the royal treasury.

Henry himself judged important cases as he travelled about the kingdom. And some of his judges sat at the palace of Westminster giving justice in the King's absence. Also, at regular intervals, *itinerant* (travelling) judges were sent 'on circuit' to each county. A few itinerant judges had been used by Henry I. But Henry II made them a permanent part of the English legal system. Nowadays their visits are known as the 'assizes'.

Before Henry's itinerant judges arrived in a county the sheriff gathered a *jury* of twelve men from the district who swore to accuse honestly all those suspected of crimes. Such 'juries of presentment' decided who they would accuse *before* coming to court. Thus they were different from the 'trial juries' we have today.

Once a man had been accused the 'ordeal' was still used to prove his guilt or innocence (see Chapter 4). Observed by a priest, he carried a red hot bar of iron or was plunged into water. The Normans introduced another method of ordeal—by battle, or *combat*. This was used to settle disputes between knights and even barons. Usually both sides were allowed to hire a 'champion' to do the fighting, so it was not a test of personal strength. As in all ordeals, God was supposed to judge who was in the right and give him the victory.

King Henry had no faith in these superstitious methods. He wanted to decide on evidence and the previous record of the accused. But it was difficult to break suddenly with the tradition of centuries. Instead Henry ruled that if an accused man with a bad reputation was lucky enough to be cleared by the ordeal he must still be banished from the kingdom! Those who failed the ordeal were punished. Even ordinary thieves could be hanged, but more often they had their eyes put out or their hands cut off.

Ordeals gave place, in time, to the modern idea of trial by jury. In 1216 the Pope, Innocent III, forbade priests from taking part in ordeals. This ruled out all but the combat, in which priests were not required.

Pope Innocent III's signature on a document

The problem of the church courts

From then on a different sort of jury was needed to decide guilt or innocence. Its members kept an open mind and heard all the evidence before giving their verdict. Juries today have the same task. Henry did not live to see this great step forward, but he did much to prepare the way. In his reign royal justice gained a reputation for fairness. More and more freemen who could afford the necessary fees willingly took their disputes to court instead of settling them violently.

The quarrel

One of Henry's main aims in reforming the law was to reduce the powers of *church courts*. These had been set up in the time of William I, to judge offences by clergymen and others against the Church and its property. Those found guilty were fined, reduced in rank or, worst of all, *excommunicated* (expelled from the Church altogether).

Excommunication was a terrible sentence for a man who took his Christian beliefs seriously. But not everyone remained true to the faith. And many bad characters claimed the right to be tried in a church court just because they were church readers or doorkeepers! Even if these men committed murder they were not put to death because the church courts could not give such a punishment.

Henry suggested that in future men found guilty of serious crimes in church courts should be handed over for further punishment in an ordinary court. Many bishops opposed him, saying that no servant of the Church should be interfered with by the King. But a chance for Henry to get his way came in 1161. Archbishop Theobald, the Head of the English Church, died. It was customary for the King to have a say in appointing church leaders, and this time Henry was determined to have a man who would support his views. The obvious choice was his close friend Thomas Becket.

Thus in 1162 Becket became Archbishop of Canterbury. So far he had shown no sign of deep religious feeling. But now he changed completely. He stayed up far into the night reading the Scriptures and rose before dawn to pray. Next to his skin he wore a rough shirt of goats' hair, swarming with lice and fleas. While costly food was served for guests and officials, Becket himself had bread and water. He was a man who did nothing by half-measures!

Becket told Henry that his duty to the Church must now come before his duty to the King. At first Henry thought he was joking. But when he found his orders challenged and his wishes ignored he realised Thomas was serious. Soon a violent quarrel broke out between them. Henry announced his intention of reforming the church courts, but Becket would have none of it. He said that if a church court expelled a man from the clergy and then handed him over to the King's court he would be punished twice for the same offence.

The King was angry and deeply hurt by Becket's attitude. He tried to settle the argument but Becket stubbornly refused to give an inch. In 1164 the Archbishop fled to the Continent and began to live the life of a monk. He poured out floods of spiteful letters which gained him more enemies than friends. Several attempts to bring peace between the two men failed.

This knocker on the door of Durham Cathedral may once have helped criminals. A suspected lawbreaker on the run often went to a church and claimed the right *sanctuary* (shelter, or refuge) to get away from those pursuing him. No one could harm him in 'God's House'. Later, when all was quiet, he could slip away—usually in the dead of night

Archbishop Thomas Becket talking to Henry II. This is taken from a thirteenth century stained glass window in the Trinity Chapel, Canterbury Cathedral

'Murder in the cathedral'

In July 1170 the King and Becket met in France. Becket got his way over the church courts and the quarrel was patched up. Early in December the Archbishop returned to England—and immediately excommunicated three bishops! He claimed they had carried out duties which only he could perform, as head of the English Church.

By this act Becket, already disliked by the nobles, made himself even more unpopular. A baron named Ranulf de Broc now began to insult him openly. He hunted over the Archbishop's estates, stole his hounds and seized a shipment of wine bound for Becket's household. Becket lost patience and on Christmas Day he excommunicated Ranulf—even though he had promised Henry that he would not harm any of his tenants-in-chief. When the news reached the King in Normandy, he flew into a rage and shouted 'Will nobody rid me of this troublesome priest?'

Four knights of his household took him at his word. Secretly they set off for England, arriving at Canterbury on 29 December. After marching into Becket's private room and threatening him they went into the garden to put on their armour. Becket's attendants persuaded him to go into the cathedral for safety. However, the knights, with swords drawn, clattered after him. They tried to drag him outside but he clung to a pillar. Suddenly there was a flurry of sword blows and Becket fell dead on the blood-spattered floor. The top of his head was almost sliced off.

Once Becket was dead his faults were forgotten. Pilgrims flocked to his tomb at Canterbury, and all sorts of miracles were reported. The blind were said to receive sight, the dumb spoke and lepers were cleansed—all by praying to Thomas, 'God's holy martyr'. In 1173 he was *canonised* (declared to be a saint) by the Pope.

The King was grief-stricken and deeply regretted his angry words. Everyone blamed him for Becket's death and waited for God to punish him. This seemed to be happening when, in 1173, his wife and his ungrateful sons Henry and Richard joined the kings of Scotland and France in a war against him. In serious danger, King Henry visited Becket's tomb the following spring to show his sorrow and repentance. He walked barefoot through the streets of Canterbury, and confessed his sins before the High Altar of the cathedral. Monks and bishops lashed his naked back with a whip.

Shortly after his pilgrimage Henry received news that his faithful barons had captured the Scottish king. A few weeks later his sons made peace. People said St Thomas had worked another miracle! Nevertheless, the last years of Henry's reign were clouded by family quarrels. Two of his sons, Henry and Geoffrey, died. But in 1189 Richard and John, together with the French king, defeated the ageing Henry and forced him to sign away some of his lands. He died in the same year, heartbroken.

Henry's friends and officials mourned his death, even if his family did not. Peter of Blois, one of his chaplains, wrote: '. . . everybody loved him, because he called for strict justice and made peace.' Outwardly he often seemed a hard and demanding ruler. But at heart he was fairminded, generous and friendly. Although Henry was a

Left: In this picture, drawn early in the thirteenth century, Becket is shown beside an altar—thus making the murder seem even more unholy

Right: Seal of Henry II

Frenchman by birth and spent more than half of his reign in France, he had great affection for his Kingdom of England. He did all in his power to restore its peace and prosperity after the bitter quarrels of Stephen's reign.

More about Henry and Becket
Pilgrimages to Becket's tomb are described in Chapter 15.

Books
M. E. Reeves, *A Medieval King Governs* (Longman, Then and There series).
Becket (Cape, History Jackdaw series, no. 98).
M. Crouch, *Canterbury* (Longman Young Books, Local History series). The section dealing with Becket and his times.

Filmstrips
Becket and His Times (Paramount, distributed by Educational Productions Ltd.). Based on 'stills' from the motion picture *Becket*.
Henry II (Rank, *Reign by Reign* series).

Visit
The tomb, or 'shrine', of St Thomas Becket at Canterbury Cathedral.

To write and find out
1 Imagine you are one of Becket's murderers. Describe the death of the Archbishop as you would tell it to a friend. Give reasons to justify what you did.
2 For future reference, list the names and dates of the 'Plantagenet' kings of England.
3 (a) How is a modern jury chosen and what are its duties? (Try to find out from someone who has done jury service.)
(b) Then write down the main differences between modern juries and those of the Middle Ages.

RICHARD · I
CŒUR · DE · LION
1189 - 1199

13   The Crusades

The crown of England passed from Henry II to his thirty-two year old son Richard. Known as *Coeur de Lion*, or 'Lion-heart', Richard I already had a reputation as a brilliant and fearless warrior. He was an impressive figure—tall, handsome and always finely dressed, unlike his father who cared little about his appearance. Richard spent most of his early life in France. So when he came to London to be crowned many of his new subjects got their first glimpse of him.

Englishmen got little chance to see him again, because he spent all but six months of his ten-year reign abroad! England became a supplier of money and men for the King's foreign wars. At the time of his coronation Richard was already preparing to go to Palestine and fight a 'crusade' against the Muslims. There had been two earlier crusades, before Richard was born. So to understand the exploits of the Lion-heart we must go back to the beginning of the story.

'God wills it!'

The Holy Land of Palestine, where Jesus once lived, came under the rule of Muslims in the seventh century. It was then that the Arab followers of Mohammed conquered all the eastern Mediterranean lands (see Chapter 5). However, the city of Jerusalem is sacred to Muslims as well as Christians. So the 'holy places' in and around the city were preserved, and Christian pilgrims from Europe were not stopped from visiting them.

In the eleventh century the situation changed. Palestine and the neighbouring countries of Syria and Asia Minor were overrun by fierce Turks from the great plains of central Asia. These Turks were Muslims, like the Arabs, but they were not so willing to live in peace with Christians. Under their rule any Christian pilgrim who entered Palestine risked his life. Some were killed, tortured or sold in the slave markets.

Further north, the Turkish conquest of Asia Minor meant Constantinople was open to attack. This great Christian city was still the capital of the Byzantine Empire, which Justinian once ruled. In 1095 its emperor, Alexius I, appealed to the Pope for assistance from Christians of the West. The Pope, Urban II, was eager to help. He thought that if Europeans united against the Turks they would stop fighting each other.

In November 1095 Pope Urban held a Church Council at Clermont in France. Speaking with great passion he urged the proud nobles and knights of Europe to go and free Byzantium and the Holy Land from the *Saracens,* as Muslims were often called. 'Christ himself will be your leader', he said. 'Wear his cross as your badge. If you are killed your sins will be pardoned.' As Urban spoke there was a great shout of *Deus le volt!* (God wills it!)

A young crusader knight. Over the top of his chainmail he wears a linen *surcoat* as a protection against the blazing sun which could make his armour uncomfortably hot. In battle he wore an iron helmet, with a metal piece covering the nose

Left: Statue of Richard I outside the Houses of Parliament

Immediately preachers travelled beyond the borders of France to gain recruits for this 'holy war'. There was no shortage of volunteers. Knights, who were trained to fight, welcomed the chance to gain heavenly salvation with their swords! Following the Pope's instructions, all volunteers sewed large crosses on their clothing. The Latin for cross is *crux,* and from this we get the word crusade (war of the cross).

Jerusalem captured

A horde of humble peasants and tradesmen set off at once for Constantinople, unorganised and unprepared. They were short of food and weapons and led not by experienced soldiers but by a monk known as Peter the Hermit. The 'People's Crusade', as it was called, had many old men, women and children in its ranks. Some of the hungry rabble died on the journey. Those who reached Asia Minor were crushed by a Turkish army (1096).

Meanwhile the real crusade got underway, led chiefly by French barons and churchmen. Well equipped armies of knights travelled eastwards from France, Germany and Italy, assembling at Constantinople in the spring of 1097. Most of them had covered 1,500 miles or more, moving wagon-loads of food, armour, weapons, tents and bedding across hot, dry plains and through snow-covered mountain passes. Not all went for religious reasons. Some hoped to gain lands for themselves, so they took their families. Others went simply for adventure or the chance to plunder the rich cities of the eastern Mediterranean.

The Emperor Alexius was not pleased when he saw the crusaders. He had expected a small, hand-picked force, ready to accept his orders. Instead he got a vast army whose main interest was in the Holy Land, not fighting to protect Byzantium. To the educated Greeks of Constantinople the crusaders seemed rough and violent. Alexius supplied them with food and then hurried them on their way to Palestine, fearing that if they stayed long they might conquer his own empire!

From Constantinople the crusaders journeyed through Asia Minor. Despite shortages of food and water they managed to defeat a Turkish army. Then came their greatest test—the mighty fortress of Antioch. The defending Saracens were well prepared and it took a siege of nearly nine months to break their resistance. Advancing down the coast, the crusaders finally reached Jerusalem in the summer of 1099.

There were frequent quarrels among the leaders, but eventually all agreed to follow the tall, handsome Duke Godfrey from Lorraine in Germany. He was not an inspiring man, but he had proved reliable and unselfish. Under his command a siege tower was made out of timber brought from the coast and the attack on Jerusalem began. It was a scorching hot July and the Saracens defended bravely. But after fifteen days of desperate fighting the crusaders swarmed across the crumbling walls. There was a terrible slaughter of Muslims and Jews inside the city.

Jerusalem was in Christian hands and all Europe rejoiced! Most of the crusaders returned home, but a few hundred knights settled on the conquered lands in Palestine and Syria. The Muslim population had to pay taxes and give half their crops to the crusader-settlers. Duke Godfrey became ruler of Jerusalem and overlord of the other Christian territories. He refused to be called king, saying he would not have a royal crown in the city where Jesus had worn the crown of thorns. But Godfrey soon died and his brother Baldwin took the title of King of Jerusalem (1100).

To help defend the new kingdom, and also to care for Christian pilgrims, two brotherhoods of 'fighting monks' were formed. These were the Knights of St John, known as the 'Hospitallers' because they kept a hospital in Jerusalem; and the Knights of the Temple, or 'Templars', whose first monastery was beside the temple in Jerusalem. The knights of both Orders took vows similar to those of monks. But instead of devoting their lives to prayer they aimed to serve God by their deeds.

The Hospitallers and Templars were too few in numbers to fight the Saracens in open battle. So they built castles and defended them. During their brief stay in Constantinople the crusaders had learnt new ways of building defences, and these were put into practice in the Christian kingdom. For example, instead of having just stone keeps they built *concentric* castles—two or three rings of walls, one

Europe and the Holy Land

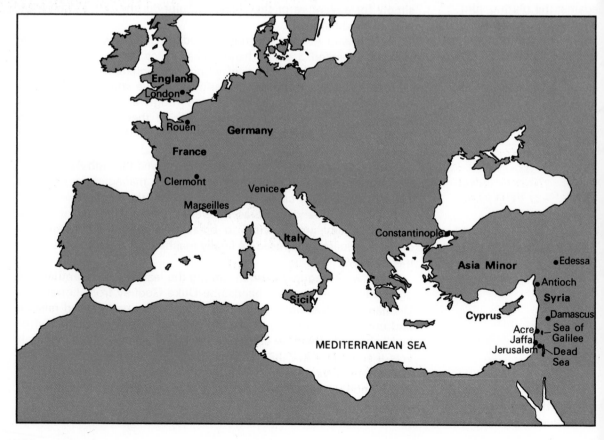

Above: The Church of the Holy Sepulchre in Jerusalem—one of the 'holy places' fought for in the crusades. It was built on the hill where Christ was crucified. Not far away lay the garden in which Christ was said to have risen from the dead

Today this eight-pointed cross is the badge of the St John Ambulance Brigade. It was originally worn by Hospitaller monks in their Hospital of St John of Jerusalem, which was founded for the medical care of pilgrims. The Hospitallers of St John later became fighting monks—Knights Hospitallers

inside the other. This idea was later introduced into Europe and can be seen in the castles built by Edward I in Wales (Chapter 16).

Sultan Saladin and the Third Crusade

The northernmost part of the Christian kingdom—Edessa and the surrounding area—was recaptured by the Saracens in 1144. This setback led to a Second Crusade, three years later, led by the French king and the emperor of Germany. But it was a disastrous failure. Most of the emperor's forces were killed or captured before the French arrived. When an attack on Damascus failed the remains of the crusading army returned home.

During the next forty years the Kingdom of Jerusalem grew steadily weaker. Finally, in 1187, the Turkish Sultan, Saladin, overwhelmed the crusader-settlers in a battle near the Sea of Galilee. Before the year was out Jerusalem and most other Christian strongholds had fallen. Saladin was hard and ruthless in battle, but he was also merciful. In contrast to the disgraceful behaviour of the crusaders when they captured Jerusalem, Saladin ordered his soldiers not to kill in the Holy City. Christians were allowed to buy their freedom.

When news of the disaster reached Europe a Third Crusade was organised. Three great monarchs prepared to go east—the Emperor Frederick I of Germany, Philip II of France and Richard I of England. To raise money for ships, soldiers and equipment Richard put heavy taxes on his subjects. Sheriffdoms and other official positions were sold to the highest bidder. Even royal lands were handed over for money. 'I would sell the city of London', said Richard, 'if only I could find a buyer.'

The crusade got off to a bad start. Frederick I was drowned while crossing a river in Asia Minor, and most of his army went back to Germany. In the meantime Richard and Philip set off together from the French port of Marseilles (1190). On the way they split up, when

Krak des Chevaliers (Castle of the Knights), one of the finest crusader castles. Notice the *concentric* walls. Built high above a mountain pass, it was much bigger than any English castle. Its garrison of 'Hospitallers' kept a year's store of food in its vaults

some English ships were blown off course to Cyprus. Richard took the opportunity of capturing the island before sailing on to Palestine. He arrived at Acre to find the other crusaders already besieging it. Some were in a poor way, suffering from fever, but Richard's appearance gave them fresh heart. Five weeks later the crusaders forced their way into Acre, using battering-rams and catapults.

The first great obstacle had been overcome, but now Philip decided he had done enough. He returned to France, leaving behind 10,000 knights under the Duke of Burgundy. Philip had no real interest in crusading, and Richard outshone him as a soldier. The two kings were really bitter rivals and had quarrelled throughout the siege of Acre. Once Philip had departed Richard was left in command of the crusade.

Saladin (Salah-ad-Din), Sultan of the Turks, 1174–93. A wise and honourable man, he was greatly admired by Christians even though he led a *jihad* (holy war) against them. Richard I had more respect for Saladin than for many of his Christian allies

King Richard's adventures

The Lion-heart led his army southwards along the coast. Plagued by swarms of flies, and suffering from thirst, hunger and disease, the crusaders bravely defeated Saladin's forces and captured Jaffa. Then, moving inland, they camped twelve miles from Jerusalem. But Richard was now so short of men and supplies that he was unable to attack it. He got to within sight of its walls, but we are told he shielded his eyes and refused to look, knowing he could not capture the Holy City.

Meanwhile, messengers brought bad news for Richard. His brother John was plotting with Philip of France and his kingdom was in danger. Anxious to get back to England, Richard made peace with Saladin in 1192. Christian armies had to give up all Palestine except a thin coastal strip about 100 miles long. In return Saladin promised to allow pilgrims to visit the holy places. This was a disappointing outcome for Richard. In the end the most valuable gain was Cyprus, which he conquered on the outward journey. It remained a Christian base against the Saracens for four centuries.

The crusaders set sail for home, but Richard's adventures did not end there. While travelling overland from Venice he was arrested on the orders of Duke Leopold of Austria. Richard and Leopold were enemies, even though they had fought together on the crusade. Richard was handed over to the German emperor, Henry VI, who claimed a vast ransom of 150,000 marks of silver. This would amount to several million pounds today.

Most of the money was paid by Richard's dutiful English subjects and he was released after thirteen months of imprisonment. He made what turned out to be his last visit to England in March 1194 and punished those who had supported his rebellious brother John. Two months later he sailed for France, where Philip had taken advantage of his absence to attack his lands. Furious at such treachery from a fellow crusader, Richard was determined to recover his losses.

One by one the Lion-heart recaptured his castles. He also built several new ones, including the massive *Chateau Gaillard* (Saucy Castle) to protect Rouen. After five years of hard fighting Richard gained the upper hand. But before he could press home his advantage he met an untimely death. Carelessly he rode without full armour near the walls of a besieged town and was struck in the shoulder by a bolt from a cross-bow. The wound turned septic and Richard died in April 1199.

The Lion-heart had neglected his kingdom and spent vast sums of money on foreign wars. Yet few kings of England were more admired by their subjects. People forgot the heavy taxes they had paid and remembered instead the courage, skill and determination of their warrior king.

A lost cause

During the next century there were several more crusades. But none met with lasting success. The religious enthusiasm of the early crusaders disappeared, and men travelled east hoping to gain lands and wealth. The Fourth Crusade never reached the Holy Land at all. Eager for plunder, an army of French knights stormed the Christian city of Constantinople (1204). For three days and nights they ransacked the churches and homes of the rich, seizing many priceless treasures. Pope Innocent III condemned the outrage, saying: 'those who . . . should have used their swords only against pagans, are dripping with the blood of Christians.'

In 1229 Jerusalem was recovered by a most unlikely crusader—the Emperor Frederick II of Germany, who admitted that he did not believe in God! Rather than fight the Saracens he made peace with them. Then, by skilful bargaining, he persuaded the Sultan to surrender the Holy City. Jerusalem remained in European hands for fifteen years, but was lost for good in 1244.

Nevertheless, King Louis IX of France led two more crusades in 1248 and 1270. In contrast to Frederick, 'St Louis', as men called

The dryness and heat of the lands the crusaders fought in can be imagined from this picture taken in modern Israel

Chateau Gaillard, completed in 1198 at a place called Les Andelys on the banks of the river Seine. Notice its *concentric* defences, copied from the crusader castles. 'I would hold it were its walls of butter', Richard is said to have boasted

him, was deeply religious. But his crusades were disastrous failures. On the first he was captured by the Saracens and had to pay a large ransom. On the second he caught a fever and died. Prince Edward of England, later Edward I, continued the crusade after Louis's death. He made a number of successful raids into Saracen territory and proved himself a good soldier. Then he agreed to a ten-year truce and sailed home.

As well as the main crusades there were many smaller expeditions, including a 'Children's Crusade' in 1212. This was led by a French shepherd boy of twelve, who believed God had chosen him to free the Holy Land from the Turks! He persuaded thousands of children to follow him to Marseilles, where some dishonest seamen promised to transport his 'army'. Some of the children died in shipwrecks. The rest were sold in the Saracen slave markets.

The last Christian stronghold in the Holy Land, the port of Acre, was captured by the Saracens in 1291. The Templars and Hospitallers, who had fought desperately to hold Acre, were forced to move their headquarters to Cyprus. But many pilgrims still travelled to the Holy Land—usually on horseback to southern Italy, by sea to the Palestine coast, and inland on foot or by donkey.

On the whole the crusades were a costly failure. They did nothing to unite the Christian rulers of Europe, whose quarrels and jealousies continued. On returning to Europe some educated crusaders helped to spread the superior knowledge of the Muslims—especially in medicine, mathematics and architecture (see Chapter 5). But this information was reaching Europe in any case through peaceful trading contacts made by the merchants of Sicily and Italy.

Timeline

1095	Pope Urban II preaches the First Crusade
1099	Jerusalem captured
1147	Second Crusade
1187	Saladin re-captures Jerusalem
1189–99	Reign of Richard I
1190–2	Third Crusade
1193–4	Richard imprisoned by the German Emperor
1204	Fourth 'Crusade' — Constantinople ransacked
1212	The Children's Crusade
1229–44	Jerusalem recovered by Frederick II
1248, 1270	The Crusades of Louis IX of France
1291	Acre falls to the Saracens

More about the Crusades

Books

A Duggan, *The Story of the Crusades* (Faber).

A. Williams, *The Crusades* (Longman, Then and There series).

J. G. and R. W. V. Gittings, *The Crusades* (Hulton, Round the World Histories).

R. R. Sellman, *The Crusades* (Methuen's Outlines series).

J. Williams, *Knights of the Crusades* (A Cassell Caravel Book).

Filmstrips

The Crusaders (Common Ground, Medieval Life).

The Crusades (Hulton).

Richard I (Rank, *Reign by Reign* series).

Ciné film

Medieval Times: The Crusades (Gateway Educational Films Ltd).

Visit

The Temple Church, London; once part of the headquarters of the Knights Templars in England, and built in the style of the Church of the Holy Sepulchre in Jerusalem.

To write and find out

1 (a) Why did the Christians of Europe believe they had a right to rule Jerusalem?

(b) Who rules it today? Make an up-to-date map of the Holy Land.

2 'Few of the crusaders behaved like Christians. In fact this "holy war" seemed to bring out the worst in those who took part.'

Write down *three* examples which support this statement and *two* which contradict it.

3 Find out about the legends of Robin Hood. What do they tell us about happenings in England during Richard's absence abroad? How much truth do you think there is in such stories?

This marble *effigy*, or image, of King John can be seen on his tomb in Worcester Cathedral. When the tomb was opened in 1797 John was found to

14 Magna Carta and the Beginning of Parliament

'John, nature's enemy.'
'He plundered his own people.'
'Cruel towards all men.'
'Hell itself is fouled by the . . . presence of John.'
'No man may ever trust him.'

These are some of the things written about King John by chroniclers, during his lifetime and shortly after his death. He is often described as the worst king ever to have sat on the English throne.

However, some historians now think this judgment is unfair. Certainly John had a very unpleasant side to his character. He was suspicious, untrustworthy and sometimes cruel. But as a king he had good qualities too. Like his father, Henry II, he was well educated, intelligent and very active in governing his kingdom. John was always on the move, regularly visiting every corner of the country. On his travels he saw that the laws were carried out, judged many disputes himself and kept a close watch on the work of royal officials.

In these ways John was a better ruler than his brother, Richard I, who neglected the kingdom. But Richard was admired for his successes on the battlefield, whereas John suffered heavy defeats. In the Middle Ages it was difficult for a king to gain respect if he failed as a warrior. In fact, John failed in most of the things he tried to do. During his reign of seventeen years (1199–1216) he was hardly ever out of trouble.

King John's troubles

John was unlucky in having to face a powerful and determined enemy—Philip II of France. It was the great ambition of Philip's life to conquer the French lands belonging to the English Crown. Richard I had needed all his military skill to drive back Philip's armies. After the Lion-heart's death Philip, gaining in strength and confidence, continued the war against John.

The English King organised his defences with great energy, but he lacked his brother's ability to lead and inspire an army. He also harmed his cause by acts of cruelty. John's teenage nephew, Arthur, Count of Brittany, was captured while fighting against his uncle. Some months later he was murdered, almost certainly at the King's orders, and some of his followers were starved to death in prison.

Many of John's French subjects joined Philip, who soon won a string of victories. In 1204 he captured *Chateau Gaillard*, Richard I's 'unconquerable' castle, and invaded Normandy. Within two years Anjou and Brittany were also in Philip's hands. Out of all the French lands ruled by his father and brother John was left with just Poitou and Gascony, part of the duchy of Aquitaine.

John never gave up hope of winning back his lands. But he needed

have been five feet five inches tall—small by modern standards, but probably about average for a man of his own day

France in the reign of John. He lost more than two-thirds of his French lands to Philip II

Philip II of France

money to fight another war, and his attempts to get it caused trouble with the barons. As feudal lord of England, the King was entitled to certain payments from his tenants. For example, when a baron died his son had to pay what was called a *relief* before he could take over his father's estate. John often demanded much larger reliefs than previous kings had done. The same happened with *scutage*—the payment kings could claim instead of military service. John asked for larger scutages, and claimed them more frequently. In all he collected as many scutages (eleven) as Henry II and Richard I put together, and in less than half the time.

There was a good reason for John's greater demands. Prices were rising rapidly during his reign. It cost him as much as two shillings a day to hire one knight, whereas his father had paid only eightpence. But the barons made no allowance for this. They accused the King of going against the 'customs of the realm'. There were no laws fixing limits to feudal payments, but each king was expected to follow the practice of previous rulers.

John also got into trouble with the Church. In 1206 he quarrelled with the Pope, Innocent III, who refused to accept his choice of a new archbishop of Canterbury. After much disagreement Innocent selected Stephen Langton, an Englishman living in his court in Rome. Stephen was well suited to the post, but John refused to have him, claiming it was usual for kings to have a say in these appointments. He was right. No English king since the Conquest had failed to get an archbishop he wanted.

Innocent would not give way. In 1208 he put England under an *interdict*, which meant all churches were locked and no services held except baptism of infants and confession for the dying. There were no marriages and no one could be buried in holy ground. This caused great distress at a time when religion was the most powerful force in people's lives. But John seemed in no hurry to settle the dispute. He seized the lands of several monasteries and forced a number of clergymen who supported the Pope to leave England. Innocent replied by *excommunicating* the King, thus making him an outcast from the Church.

Not until 1213 did John give in and accept Langton, who ended the excommunication. The interdict was lifted the following year, and all over the kingdom people rejoiced to hear again the peal of church bells. John's quarrel with the Pope partly explains the nasty things written about him at the time. He did not, in fact, hate the Church. But monks, who wrote most of the chronicles, believed that a king who was excommunicated must be an evil monster.

The seal of Archbishop Stephen Langton

Baronial rebellion

John made a determined effort to recover his French lands in the summer of 1214. On his side was the German Emperor, Otto IV, who agreed to attack King Philip from the north while John came up from the south. But Philip defeated Otto at Bouvines, in Flanders, and the plan was ruined. John returned to England, short of money, to face a baronial rebellion.

A powerful group of barons had been plotting against John for some time. Many had been forced to pay vast sums of money to the King, and some had been denied proper justice in his court. Now the time had come for a showdown. If John had been victorious in France he could have stood up to them. But when he failed a second time he lost the support of a number of barons who had previously been faithful.

Hoping to prevent bloodshed, Archbishop Stephen Langton got the rebels to draw up a list of grievances and present them to the King. These accused him of ignoring certain customs established by past kings and demanded that he must make a solemn promise to keep to them in future. John was furious! Never before had an English king been expected to obey written rules, and he had no intention of being the first to do so. When their demands were rejected the barons decided to use force. In April 1215 they gathered their armed knights at Stamford in Lincolnshire and began marching south.

John still had some support. Most of the sheriffs remained loyal. So did his *constables* (in charge of the royal castles) and a few of the greatest barons—including William Marshal, Earl of Pembroke, one of the most respected men in England. Nevertheless John could not

This map shows the position of Runnymede, where John met the barons. It was low-lying and frequently flooded. So it was almost an island between the Thames and a small lake which had once been part of the old course of the river

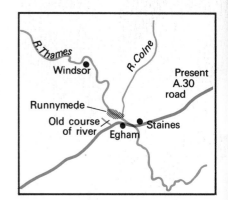

prevent the rebels from occupying London. He fled to Windsor Castle and asked for peace, knowing it was useless to resist any longer. On 15 June a meeting between the two sides took place in a meadow called Runnymede, beside the River Thames between Staines and Windsor.

The Great Charter

Discussions went on for several days at Runnymede before the terms of peace were agreed. Then everything that the King had promised was written in Latin on a piece of parchment, and a wax impression of the Great Seal was attached to it. This document, the most important in all English history, became known as *Magna Carta* (Latin for 'the Great Charter').

Many copies of the Great Charter were made by royal clerks in the summer of 1215. They were sent to sheriffs and other important officials, so that all leading subjects could be told what the King had granted. Only four of these copies exist today—one in Lincoln

One of the two copies of *Magna Carta* in the British Museum, London. (The other was damaged by fire in 1731.) This copy measures $20\frac{1}{4}$ inches by $13\frac{1}{2}$, and probably took a clerk the best part of a day to write out. Such charters did not have paragraphs, but it is usual to divide *Magna Carta* into sixty-three short sections

One side of John's Great Seal, showing him sitting on his throne. Every copy of *Magna Carta* carried a wax impression of this seal, which measures just over $3\frac{1}{2}$ inches across. Such documents were sealed to show they were genuine. Nowadays we simply write our signature

Cathedral, one in Salisbury Cathedral and two in the British Museum.

Magna Carta was granted to all freemen of England. But the barons gained most from it. They aimed to make John rule according to the 'customs of the realm'. So they got him to set out in the Charter what they believed these customs to be.

In future John was not to ask for scutage until his tenants-in-chief had agreed to it. And the relief a baron had to pay when he inherited his father's lands was fixed at £100 (some had paid several thousand pounds earlier in John's reign!). Knights also benefited from the Charter, because it said barons must grant to their own tenants what the King was granting them. Thus the relief of a knight was fixed at £5—the usual amount in Henry II's time.

Next to regulations about money payments the most important parts of Magna Carta were to do with justice. John had considered the giving of justice to be a personal favour, which he could refuse if he wanted to. He made some unfortunate barons pay large sums of money just to get a fair trial! In future, no freeman was

to be punished without a proper trial and the King was not to sell or deny justice to anyone.

The Charter granted many more baronial demands. For example, the royal forests were to be reduced in size; certain unpopular sheriffs and foreign judges were to be dismissed, and the English Church was to be free to obey the Pope. A committee of twenty-five barons was chosen to keep a check on the King. They were ready to use force if he broke his promises. But although the Charter allowed this committee to be formed John had no intention of taking orders from it. He preferred to fight rather than allow barons to sit in judgment on him. So in September 1215 civil war broke out again.

With borrowed money John hired soldiers from the Continent and put up a strong resistance. But he did not live to see the end of the fighting. In the night of 18 October 1216, he died suddenly at Newark in Nottinghamshire, after heavy eating and drinking. 'At his end', wrote a chronicler, 'few mourned for him.' However, John's death did not mean Magna Carta was forgotten. It became part of the law of the land and in the years ahead barons made sure kings remembered what it said.

Bronze figure of Henry III in Westminster Abbey

Earl Simon's Parliament

John's nine-year old son was crowned King Henry III, and a group of loyal barons began to govern the country until the boy was old enough to rule himself. The civil war soon ended and a new version of Magna Carta was issued which included most of the things granted by John. For the time being the barons seemed satisfied and the kingdom was at peace.

Henry grew up into a kind and gentle man. He had a good education and loved books, painting and architecture. But although he was more pleasant than his father he lacked strength and firmness. He allowed his French wife, Eleanor, to crowd his court with her friends and relations. Many of these foreigners were given large estates and important positions in the King's government. Henry even allowed the Pope to appoint about 300 foreign clergymen to English churches.

The English barons and Church leaders complained bitterly. They were supposed to be the King's advisers, yet he took little notice of them, preferring to listen to his foreign courtiers. In 1258 the English barons finally lost patience. They met at Oxford and demanded changes in the way the country was being governed. Henry was forced to hand over most of his power to a council of fifteen barons, led by Simon de Montfort, Earl of Leicester.

Unfortunately the barons soon began to argue amongst themselves. Some were jealous of Earl Simon's power and encouraged Henry to oppose the council of fifteen. 'Servants should not judge their masters', said the King. But when he raised an army to punish the rebels he was defeated and taken prisoner (1264).

For a while Simon de Montfort was practically the ruler of England. He assembled Great Councils just as though he was a king. But many nobles refused to co-operate with him. So to gain wider support Simon tried an experiment in January 1265 which was to have important consequences for the future. He held a Great Council to

Parliament in the days of Edward I, showing the King with his tenants-in-chief. The King sat on a raised throne, near his Treasurer, Chancellor and other royal officials. Llewellyn, Prince of Wales, and King Alexander of Scotland are also present on this occasion. The 'Commons', if they were invited, did not sit with the Great Council. After a brief speech by the Chancellor they left the main hall to discuss the King's proposals among themselves

Aussi se ledit colier dor avoit besoing de reparacion il pora
estre mis en la main de souurier iusques a ce quil soit
repare. Lequel colier aussi ne pourra estre enrichy de
pierres ou daultres choses reserue ses ymage qui pourra
estre garny au plaisir du cheualier. Et aussi ne pourra
estre ledit colier vendu engaige donne ne aliene pour
necessite ou cause quelconque que ce soit

Alexander Rex
Scotor

le bethin
princeps
wallie

which he invited not only the nobles who supported him but also the representatives of ordinary freemen. Each county was asked to send two knights, and each town that was friendly to him sent two *burgesses* (citizens).

Never before had tenants-in-chief been joined by both knights and townsmen to discuss the government of the realm. But if it was the first time it was certainly not the last. This sort of assembly later came to be called a *Parliament*. Simon's main support was among the knights and burgesses—that is why he invited them. But their presence was also a sign of the growing influence of lesser landowners and town merchants in the affairs of the kingdom.

King, Lords and Commons

The rule of Simon de Montfort came to a sudden end in the summer of 1265. Many of his followers changed sides and he was defeated by Prince Edward, the King's eldest son, in a bloody battle at Evesham in Worcestershire. Outnumbered and penned in against the banks of the River Avon, all the rebel leaders were slaughtered. Simon's dead body was cut into pieces by a knight who had earlier supported him.

Prince Edward, strong and vigorous, took over from his ageing father and promised to rule according to Magna Carta. Seven years later Henry died and Edward became king in his own right (1272–1307). Although he had restored the power of the Crown, Edward I set out to rule with the help and agreement of his subjects. He took up Simon de Montfort's idea and from time to time (beginning in 1275) he invited knights and burgesses to attend his Great Council of nobles. He listened to their complaints and asked them to agree, in the name of the people, to the collection of certain taxes.

Such gatherings gave the King and his subjects a chance to *parley* (talk) and this is how we get the word Parliament. Meetings of Parliament could take place anywhere, but they were usually held in the hall of the royal palace at Westminster. The modern Houses of Parliament stand on the same site, close by the banks of the Thames.

In Edward's reign, and for a long time afterwards, the barons and bishops of the Great Council (known as 'the Lords') were the most powerful members of Parliament. The knights and burgesses (known as 'the Commons') were only invited on special occasions at first. But their control of taxation made them increasingly important. In time two separate Houses of Parliament developed—the Lords and Commons.

As well as agreeing to taxation, the Commons presented *petitions* (requests) to the King. If he agreed to a petition he wrote on it, in French, 'le roi le veult' (the king wills it) and it then became law. Such petitions were the first Parliamentary Bills. When a Bill becomes law nowadays the monarch's approval is still written in French.

In the Middle Ages Parliament only met when it was called by the King. Its task was to give advice not make decisions on its own. There were no political parties, and no one thought of asking peasants and other lesser folk to elect members to represent them in Parliament. Only people with property were thought fit to take part in governing. Not until quite recent times did Parliament take the form it has today.

Simon de Montfort, taken from a window in Chartres Cathedral in France

Timeline
A.D.
1199–1216 Reign of John
1204   Loss of Normandy to Philip II
1208–14   England under an interdict
1215   Magna Carta
1216–72   Reign of Henry III
1265   Simon de Montfort's Parliament
1272–1307 Reign of Edward I

More about Magna Carta and Parliament

Books

J. C. Holt, *Magna Carta* (Longman, Then and There series).

C. W. Hodges, *Magna Carta* (O.U.P., Story of Britain series).

King John and Magna Carta (Cape, History Jackdaw series, no. 3).

D. Scott-Daniell, *Battles and Battlefields* (Batsford). Chapter 3 for the battle of Evesham, 1265.

A translation of *Magna Carta* can be obtained from Her Majesty's Stationery Office.

Filmstrip

John (Rank, *Reign by Reign* series).

Ciné Film

Magna Carta, Parts 1 and 2 (Encyclopaedia Brittanica, distributed by Gaumont British). Especially Part 2: 'Revolt of the Nobles and the Signing of the Charter'.

Visits

Runnymede, where there is a museum and a memorial to *Magna Carta*. John's tomb at Worcester Cathedral.

To write

1 An imaginary conversation between King John and Archbishop Stephen Langton at Runnymede. (The Archbishop is trying to persuade John to agree to the barons' demands, but the King is angry and very stubborn.)

2 How did Parliament in the time of Edward I differ from:
   (a) the Norman Great Council?
   (b) the Anglo-Saxon Witan? (turn back to Chapter 4, second section).

3 John was Henry II's favourite son, and his father would have preferred to see him rule ahead of Richard.

   If Henry had come back to life after 1216 what do you think he would have said about the reigns of his sons? Would he have changed his preference for John? (Remember to give reasons for your views.)

15   The Catholic Church

Today there are many different sorts of Christians. In England alone we find Anglicans (Church of England), Methodists, Quakers, Baptists, Catholics and many others. But in the Middle Ages all the Christians of Europe belonged to one Catholic (universal) Church, headed by the Pope in Rome. An English visitor to the Continent found the Mass and the other Latin services no different from those he knew at home.

In every Christian country wealthy men hoped to save their souls by giving land and money to build churches and monasteries. So over the centuries the Church grew rich and became the largest landowner in Europe. It collected its own taxes and made its own laws—called *canon law*. But the real strength of the Church was its power over men's minds.

A medieval parish church, at Syleham, Suffolk. In medieval times there were no stools or pews inside, only a few stone benches along the walls. Thus most of the congregation stood or knelt

A purpose in life

It is difficult for us to understand how much the Christian faith meant to medieval people. Frequent plagues, diseases, famines and wars cut short millions of lives. Death was closer and somehow more real than it is today, and people thought about it a lot. They looked for a purpose and meaning in life, and found it in Christianity. The Church taught that death was merely a gateway to eternal happiness for those who followed the teachings of Christ.

The parish church was a constant reminder to people of their duties to God. Every day peasants working in the fields heard its bells and saw its tower, rising high above their flimsy wooden huts. In that same solid stone church they had been baptised and perhaps married, and in its holy ground they would finally be buried. On Sundays and holy-days throughout the year everyone attended mass. The church and its churchyard were even used for meetings and celebrations, so it was truly the centre of community life.

Churches were built not just to hold congregations but also to glorify God. So they were larger than they needed to be, often with room for two or three times the number of people in the parish. The worshippers gathered in the main body of the church, called the *nave*. The end where the priest performed mass at the altar (the *chancel*) was kept private. As England became more prosperous, the naves of many churches were enlarged with side aisles, to allow more space for religious processions. Stained glass windows and rich altar decorations were added in the wealthiest parishes.

To a humble peasant or tradesman, living in a cramped and smelly hut, the parish church must have seemed like another world—spacious and peaceful. As he stood or knelt on the stone floor, statues, carvings and colourful wall paintings reminded him of the joys of heaven and the torments of hell. Perhaps an imaginary scene from the Last

Christ on the cross—from the Church of St Michael, Beetham, Westmorland

Judgment was depicted on the walls, showing devils tormenting the souls of the damned. Few worshippers understood the Latin mass. But the strangeness of the words only increased their feeling of awe and wonder.

Priests and bishops

The parish priest lived by himself, for it was a law of the Church that no clergyman could marry. Instead of having his own family the priest was supposed to devote himself to the needs of all people in the parish. If he was conscientious there was plenty to keep him busy, apart from holding the daily services.

The priest was expected to visit the sick and help the poor. He also taught his parishoners the little they knew about Christianity. He got them to learn the Ten Commandments, a few simple prayers and common Bible stories like those of Adam and Eve and Noah's Ark. If he was sufficiently educated himself he taught Latin and Scripture to a few boys in the parish, and trained them to assist with church services. In time such pupils might themselves become priests.

To support himself, a priest charged fees for baptisms, weddings and burials. In a village parish he also had some farming land, called the *glebe,* which usually included strips in the open fields. Priests took a *tithe* (tenth) of everyone's produce; but most of this went to the bishop, for the benefit of the Church. About a quarter was kept in the parish to aid the poor, the sick and the elderly. Country folk paid tithes in crops and animals. Town craftsmen and traders paid a tenth of the value of goods they made and sold.

Parishes were grouped together into dioceses, each governed by a

Canterbury Cathedral today. Cathedrals were usually shaped like a cross, with the short arms, or *transepts*, facing north and south. The nave was to the west, while the part called the *choir* stretched eastwards to the altar. Both nave and choir were divided into aisles by pillars supporting the roof

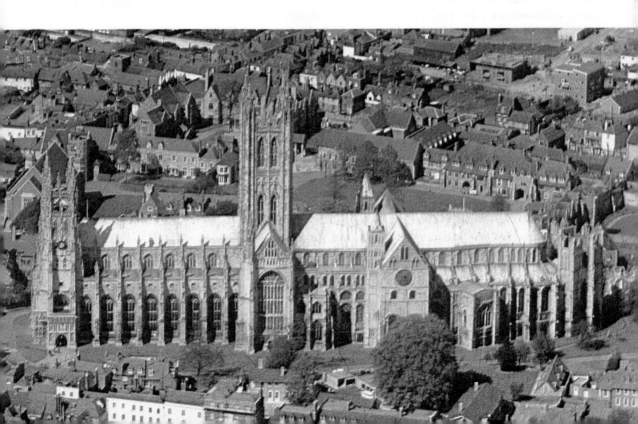

bishop. The bishop's church, usually large and impressive, was the cathedral—so called because it contained his *cathedra*, or throne. A bishop was responsible for the good behaviour of clergymen in his diocese, and wrongdoers were punished in his church court. He also performed sacraments, or religious ceremonies, such as confirmation and *holy orders* (by which men were made priests). A diocese might cover two or three counties, so the bishop could not visit every parish personally. He was often represented by his assistant, the archdeacon —known as the 'bishop's eye'.

In Saxon times bishops lived quietly and simply. But after the Norman Conquest they became almost princely figures, with large estates, fine palaces and many servants. Bishops were feudal tenants-in-chief of the king and thus occupied with affairs of government. They attended the king's Great Council, and some acted as ambassadors to foreign courts. Most bishops were well educated and hardworking, but their grand style of living put them out of touch with humble priests and their parishoners.

New orders of monks

The founding of the Benedictine order of monks in the sixth century has been described in Chapter 2. St Benedict's *Rule*, written to guide the brothers' daily work and prayer, was followed in monasteries all over Europe. For hundreds of years the Benedictines set a good example of plain Christian living and encouraged learning and education. But in time most abbeys relaxed their rules. Many monks became idle and lived comfortably, with soft beds and plenty of food.

Some of the more devoted monks longed to return to the stern, simple ways of the early Benedictines. So small groups broke away and founded new 'reformed orders'. The first of these—the *Cluniacs*—started at the French abbey of Cluny in 910. Its monks followed Benedict's *Rule* very closely.

Much stricter were the *Carthusians*, who lived alone in separate cells, silently reading and praying. The Carthusian order began in the eleventh century when seven monks went to live high upon Mount Chartreuse, near Grenoble in France. They fasted, dressed in rough garments and only left their solitary cells to meet for church services. This hard way of life was never popular in England, where only ten Carthusian monasteries were established.

By far the largest new order—the *Cistercians*—also originated in France, at the abbey of Citeaux (pronounced *Seetoe*) in 1098. St Benedict taught that 'to work is to pray', so the Cistercians gave much time to working with their hands. They built monasteries in wild, lonely places and set out to clear forest and scrubland. Cistercians wore habits of undyed wool and were thus known as the 'White Monks' (Benedictines were called 'Black Monks', from their black tunic and hood).

Groups of White Monks soon came to England and settled mostly in the lonely hills and dales of the North and West. In Yorkshire, where they built the famous abbeys of Rievaulx and Fountains, they farmed lands that had been deserted since William I's 'harrying of the North'. The Cistercians turned hillsides into rich sheep pastures and produced

Above: A Benedictine monk, and,
Above right: A Cistercian monk
Despite the appearance of several 'reformed' orders, the Benedictines remained the largest Order of monks throughout the Middle Ages

great quantities of wool. This they sold to pay for necessities such as salt, candles, iron and building materials.

The farming estates of most Cistercian abbeys grew so large that the monks could not manage by themselves. Much of the work was done by *lay brothers*—men who wanted to serve God but lacked the education necessary to become monks. Hundreds of lay brothers lived in the largest Cistercian abbeys, praying, eating and sleeping in separate quarters.

The first White Monks lived in rough wooden huts and built bare stone churches. But with the profits from wool sales craftsmen were hired to rebuild monasteries and put up magnificent churches. Apart from the Carthusians, who had individual cells, all other monastic orders kept to much the same layout of buildings—shown in the plan of Fountains Abbey.

The church was normally the largest building. Tucked into the sheltered corner formed by its south transept and nave was the *cloister*—a square covered passageway usually surrounding a lawn. Here the monks spent several hours a day, walking, reading and praying. Most of the main buildings led into the cloister. The rest of the area within the outer walls (not shown on the plan) was dotted with barns, stables, workshops, a bakehouse, brewery, mill and fish-ponds. Near the main gate was an *almonry*, where poor people could get free food and clothing.

According to Benedict's *Rule* the brothers were supposed to attend eight services of praise each day, including one in the middle of the

Right: Medieval painting showing nuns at a service. Nuns made the same vows (promises) as monks and worshipped in similar ways. About half the convents in England followed the Benedictine Rule, but instead of working in the fields or studying they did spinning and needlework. Many women only became nuns because they failed to find a husband!

Fountains Abbey, a Cistercian
monastery near
Ripon in Yorkshire
Above: Aerial view
Below: Plan

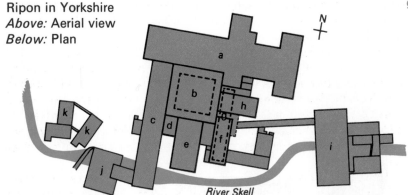

River Skell

a CHURCH
b CLOISTER
c LAY BROTHERS' REFECTORY
(dining hall) and STOREROOMS
below. LAY BROTHERS'
DORMITORY above.
d KITCHEN
e REFECTORY, or dining hall.
Similar to the hall of a manor
house, with the abbot's high
tables and stools and trestle
tables for the monks. In one
wall was a pulpit from which
one of the monks read aloud
during meals.

f MONKS' DAY ROOM (below)
with DORMITORY over it,
extending above the Chapter
House to the church. The monks
slept on straw mattresses
covered with rough woollen
blankets. A flight of stone
steps ('night stairs') led from
the Dormitory straight into
the church. So the monks
could attend the night service
without having to go into the
cold cloister.

g PARLOUR—a little room where
the monks were allowed to
talk. (Silence was the rule in
the cloister and other
buildings.) It got its name
from the French word *parler*
(to speak).

h CHAPTER HOUSE, or
assembly hall, where
the abbot held
meetings of the whole
community—to give orders
and sometimes to punish
monks who broke the rules. A
chapter of the Rule was read
at each assembly—hence the
name of the building.
i INFIRMARY (hospital) for
sick and aged monks, and
other sick people from the
neighbourhood.
j LAY BROTHERS' INFIRMARY
k (hospital).
GUEST HOUSES for travellers
and pilgrims. Guests were not
allowed in any buildings
round the cloister.

night. But as monasteries got bigger, monks were often so busy that they missed services. Cistercian abbeys in particular were like large farming businesses, with numerous fields of crops and thousands of sheep, cattle and pigs. While lay brothers did most of the farming the monks managed the storehouses, did book-keeping and sold their produce at market. Regular journeys to markets meant the end of the rule forbidding monks to go outside their monastery. Before long they were leaving the cloisters on the slightest excuse and travelling freely in the outside world.

St Francis and the friars

Monks tried to serve God while living apart from their fellow men. But Francis Bernadone, son of a rich merchant from Assisi in Italy, thought differently. He remembered Christ's command to the Twelve Apostles that they must go out into the world and teach the people. In 1207, when he was about twenty-five, Francis gave up his comfortable home to live like one of Christ's disciples. Clothed in beggar's rags he tramped the roads of Italy, preaching and helping anyone in trouble.

St Francis of Assisi, as we now call him, was a kind and gentle man. He loved animals, birds and all living creatures, and taught men to love one another. Many devoted followers gave up all their possessions to join Francis and become his *friars* (brothers). Homeless and penniless, they begged for food and shelter as they travelled from place to place. Soon missions were organised to countries outside Italy, and in 1224 the first group of shabby, barefooted *Franciscans* arrived in England.

Meanwhile a second order of friars—the *Dominicans*—was founded by St Dominic, a Spaniard who went to preach in France. Unlike St Francis he was a scholar who had trained for the Church and studied at university. But he admired the simple, holy ways of the Italian and tried to follow his example. Many Dominicans were outstanding writers and teachers, so they gained a reputation for their learning. A small group arrived in England three years before the first Franciscans.

Friars preached in the streets and market places, as well as parish churches. They went into the poorest quarters of towns, ignoring the dirt and dangers of disease, to care for the sick and unfortunate. Dominicans especially were much more educated than ordinary priests. Crowds flocked to hear their sermons, which were often witty and full of entertaining stories. Both Orders gained hundreds of new recruits, and before long the wandering friar was a familiar sight on the highways of England.

Unfortunately, like the monks, friars found it hard to remain poor and humble. They too were given lands by rich men and built themselves comfortable friaries to live in. To keep up their higher standard of living they put more effort into begging. A few brothers in each friary became almost full-time beggars, collecting food, clothing and even money—which St Francis had strictly forbidden. But despite their failings the friars aroused a new interest in Christianity and, by founding schools, did much to advance education.

Nineteenth century pictures of the two orders of friars. The Franciscan (above) wears a simple grey robe, tied at the waist by a rope. From their dress Franciscans were known as 'Grey Friars'. On the other hand St Dominic's followers (pictured below) were known as the 'Black Friars', from their black cloak and hood

137

Woodcut showing a grammar school class. Notice that the master has his birch ready to hand. These pupils have books of their own, but this was unusual in most medieval schools

Books were so valuable in the Middle Ages that it was normal in libraries to find them chained to the shelves, as shown in this picture from Hereford Cathedral

Medieval schools

Education, in the sense of book-learning, was almost entirely in the hands of the Church. Teachers were nearly all monks, friars and priests—men who had taken *holy orders*. Indeed, religion and education were so closely linked that if a man was called a clerk it meant both that he was a churchman and that he could read and write.

There were no primary schools to teach basic reading and writing. But parents who could afford it hired clergymen to act as private tutors to their children. Some wealthy families put their daughters into convents, to be taught by nuns, and packed their sons off to serve as pages in a neighbouring household. A page had lessons from the family chaplain. But good manners, and the ability to ride, hunt and fight were thought more important than book-learning in the preparation for knighthood.

Most ordinary working folk knew nothing of reading and writing. But a few peasants' sons had lessons from the local priest. They learned Bible stories and a little Latin to help them follow the church services. Some were rewarded with a minor position in the parish church, such as bellringer or door-keeper.

For more advanced education, rich and poor alike had to get a thorough knowledge of Latin in a school that taught grammar. Latin was then a living language, written and spoken all over Europe by scholars, lawyers and even merchants. Most 'grammar schools' were attached to cathedrals, friaries and large churches. Monastery schools also taught grammar. They were really intended for *novices* (those preparing to become monks) but other pupils were occasionally taught as well.

Grammar schools were small, usually with just one teacher and perhaps twenty or thirty boys in a single classroom. The pupils studied for about nine hours a day, starting soon after sunrise. They worked on Saturdays and often on Sunday mornings too. But there were holidays for saints' feast days and usually a longer break at Christmas and Easter. There were no organised games, and no lessons in English, history, geography, science and other subjects familiar nowadays. Nearly all the time was spent reading, writing and speaking Latin.

Books were scarce and very expensive because all were hand-written. In most classes the teacher had the only copy of the book being studied. So pupils had to learn everything by heart. Their attention must often have wandered, and when it did they were flogged with birch rods. It was believed that the best way to make children learn was to birch them for every mistake.

Surprisingly, many boys grew to love learning, despite the dull teaching and frequent beatings. When they had mastered Latin many went on to arithmetic, geometry and astronomy. Teachers of advanced subjects such as divinity, law and medicine were few and far between. They gathered together in two or three towns, which quickly gained reputations as centres of learning.

This was how the universities of Oxford and Cambridge started, early in the thirteenth century. Oxford, the first and largest, grew rapidly when its famous teachers of divinity and law were joined by Franciscan and Dominican friars. Carrying their possessions in bundles, students came from far and wide to study there. Some were as young as fourteen or fifteen, yet they had to find their own lodgings and look after themselves in a strange town. There were many older students too—mostly clergymen studying for degrees, which took many years to complete.

Medieval scholars were not encouraged to think for themselves or find out more about the world. The writings of the ancient Greeks and Romans, and the teachings of the early Church Fathers were accepted without question. One of the few to criticise this attitude towards learning was Roger Bacon (1210—90), an Oxford scholar and teacher. He said educated men should seek to find out new truths by making their own investigations and experiments.

One of Bacon's chief interests was astronomy. He collected many

Popular places of pilgrimage in England

a WESTMINSTER ABBEY
Shrine of King Edward the Confessor — made a saint in the twelfth century.

b CANTERBURY CATHEDRAL
Shrine of Archbishop Thomas Becket, murdered in 1170.

c ST ALBANS CATHEDRAL
Built on the hill where St Alban, the first Christian martyr in England, was executed by the Romans in the third century, A.D.

d BURY ST EDMUNDS in Suffolk. Tomb of King Edmund of East Anglia — killed by the Danes in the time of Alfred the Great.

e WALSINGHAM in Norfolk, a famous statue of the Virgin Mary.

f DURHAM CATHEDRAL
The shrine of St Cuthbert, a much loved abbot of Lindisfarne and bishop of Northumbria in the seventh century.

scientific instruments and built himself an observatory for studying the planets and stars. Unfortunately his refusal to believe all he was told got him into trouble with the Church. He was accused of doubting some of its teachings about the universe and imprisoned in 1272. So strong was Bacon's belief that man could master nature that he fore-told some of the great inventions of modern times. He said that one day there would be mechanically-driven ships and piloted flying machines!

Pilgrimages

A pilgrimage is a journey to a place thought particularly holy. In the Middle Ages people went on pilgrimages for all sorts of reasons. Some wanted their sins to be forgiven, others prayed for a very special favour or simply gave thanks to God. Over the centuries thousands of

Sixteenth century picture of pilgrims leaving the walled city of Canterbury

The Canterbury Tales

pilgrims from Europe visited the Holy Land, where Christ lived and died. But most Christians, unable to make such a long journey, were attracted to holy places nearer home.

A number of churches in England and on the Continent had sacred *shrines* (burial caskets or tombs) containing the bodies of saints or their relics, such as bits of bone, hair or clothing. It was widely believed that shrines had special powers, particularly the power of healing. So people suffering from diseases such as leprosy journeyed to kiss a saint's tomb in the hope of being cured.

Some English pilgrims visited the churches of Rome, which contained the shrines of St Peter, St Paul and many more famous saints. Others went to Compostella in Spain, where St James was believed to be buried. But most English pilgrims visited shrines in their own country. Six of the most popular are shown on the map. Of these, the shrine of St Thomas Becket attracted the largest number of visitors. During the spring and summer, when travelling was easiest, thousands of pilgrims crowded the roads to Canterbury. The wealthy ones rode horses, but most went on foot. They wore sandals, long cloaks and sometimes round, wide-brimmed hats if the sun was strong.

Just as people today go on organised tours, so in the Middle Ages pilgrims often travelled in groups. We have a wonderful description of one such journey in *The Canterbury Tales,* written in the fourteenth century by the famous poet Geoffrey Chaucer. English was then beginning to replace Latin in the writing of stories and poems, although the language Chaucer used was different from our English today!

The poet tells how a party of thirty pilgrims set out from London to visit Becket's shrine. To pass the time they tell each other stories as they ride along. These make up the bulk of Chaucer's poem, but he also describes each of the pilgrims. He must have been on a journey of this kind himself and drawn his characters from real life. Among them are people of many different occupations—a much-travelled knight and his squire, a merchant, a friar, an Oxford scholar, a miller, priest, cook, doctor, monk and many more.

Chaucer's opinion of his religious characters is very interesting. He admired the priest because he practised what he preached. He had few possessions, 'But riche he was of hooly thoght and werk'. However, Chaucer poked fun at the other churchmen because they did not live as strictly as they should. The fat monk was fonder of the hunting field than of the cloister:

'Grehoundes he hadde as swift as fowel in flight;
Of prikyng (riding) and of huntyng for the hare
Was al his lust (desire), for no cost wolde he spare.'

Similarly, the friar was a worldly man who seemed to care more for pleasure than his service to God:

'He knew the tavernes wel in every toun
And everich hostiler (innkeeper) and tappestere (barmaid)
Bet than a lazar (leper) or a beggestere (beggar).'

Chaucer on his horse— from an illustrated manuscript of *The Canterbury Tales.* Geoffrey Chaucer (1340–1400) was the son of a London merchant. For a time he worked in the service of King Edward III. He travelled abroad, and was once a Member of Parliament for the county of Kent. His wide experience helped him to become one of England's greatest poets

At the time Chaucer was writing, the strict rules of St Benedict and St Francis were often ignored. Monks and friars still praised God and did good works. But they also expected to have possessions of their own, to dress smartly and enjoy sports and other worldly pleasures.

More about the medieval Church

See Chapter 20 for later criticisms of the Church.

Books

E. Vale, *Churches,* and *Cathedrals* (Batsford, Junior Heritage series).

M. E. Reeves, *The Medieval Monastery* (Longman, Then and There series).

C. Northcote, *A Twelfth Century Benedictine Nun* (O.U.P., People of the Past).

E. Nunn, *English Monasteries* (Ginn's History Bookshelves, Green Shelf).

E. W. Grierson, *St Francis of Assisi* (Mowbray).

G. Evans, *Learning in Medieval Times* (Longman, Then and There series).

The Canterbury Tales (Penguin Classics, tr. by N. Coghill).

Filmstrips

The Monastery (Common Ground, Medieval Life).

The Medieval World (Longman, Then and There Filmstrips). No. 1 for Religious life.

Ciné Films

The Medieval Monastery (Gaumont British Film Library).

Chaucer's England (Encyclopaedia Britannica, distrib, Rank).

Visit

The ruins of a Cistercian monastery in England. Examples include Tintern (Monmouthshire), Rievaulx and Fountains (Yorkshire). Buckfast Abbey (Devon) has been rebuilt on the original site.

To write and find out

1 Imagine you are a fourteen-year-old student and you have been at Oxford only a few weeks. Write a letter to your parents telling them all your news since you left home. (Try to find out how such letters were delivered in the Middle Ages.)

2 What were the chief differences between monks and friars? Which would you have chosen to be, and why?

3 Nowadays Catholics from many countries go on a pilgrimage to Lourdes in France. Find out what happened at Lourdes that makes people want to go there.

16   Edward I, Wales and Scotland

When the English invaded Britain, back in the fifth and sixth centuries, their advance was halted at the uplands of the North and West. The Scottish and Welsh hill folk grew up as separate peoples, sharing the mainland of Britain with the English. The Irish too, separated by sea, kept their own rulers, language and traditions.

In later centuries armies from England tried to conquer the outlying parts of the British Isles. They had little success in Ireland. Henry II invaded its eastern shores in 1171 but his efforts were not followed up. By the end of the Middle Ages only Dublin and the surrounding area remained under the rule of the English Crown. However, Wales and Scotland, unprotected by sea, faced frequent attacks from the neighbouring English.

It was in the reign of Edward I (1272–1307) that the English made their greatest assault on Welsh and Scottish freedom. 'Warlike as a leopard, Edward shines out like a new Richard', wrote one of his subjects. But unlike Richard I, who fought mostly in France, Edward tried to master the mainland of Britain.

Coin showing Edward I— known as 'Longshanks' because he was very tall. A wise and firm ruler, who called Parliaments and cared much for order and justice, Edward was also an outstanding soldier and more religious than most medieval kings. He went on a Crusade in 1270 and would have gone a second time if he had been less occupied with problems at home

Wales in the time of Edward I

Llewellyn, Lord of Snowdonia

The Welsh were a warlike people, living in a rugged, mountainous land. There were very few areas flat enough to be ploughed and sown with crops. In these parts—near the coast, along river valleys and on the Isle of Anglesey—farmers settled in villages. But up in the hills there lived scattered tribes of herdsmen, with their cattle, sheep and goats. As they wandered from place to place in search of fresh pastures, these wild, restless folk constantly fought each other. Brave deeds in war were remembered in the ballads of minstrels called *bards,* who sang in the halls of tribal chiefs.

King Offa's dyke (see Chapter 4) kept the Welsh and English apart in Saxon times, except for border raids by cattle rustlers. But the Norman Conquest of England brought changes. To guard the border country, known as the *Welsh Marches,* William I gave large estates to the earls of Chester, Shrewsbury and Hereford. These 'marcher lords' and their descendants began to advance across the frontier into central and southern Wales. But in the mountainous North-West, topped by the peak of Snowdon, the Welsh chiefs were still free and determined to fight back.

When Edward I became king, Snowdonia—or *Gwynedd* as the Welsh called it—was ruled by a powerful chief named Llewellyn. He had recently re-conquered most of central Wales from the marcher lords and forced all the lesser Welsh chiefs to obey him. Now there were signs that Llewellyn had still greater ambitions. In a treaty made with Edward's father, Henry III, Llewellyn had agreed to pay homage to the English King as his overlord. But when Edward came to the throne the Lord of Snowdonia missed the coronation ceremony and proudly refused to renew his homage.

After several reminders had brought excuses from Llewellyn, Edward declared war. In 1277 he led an army along the north coast of Wales, while the marcher lords advanced further south. Llewellyn retired to the safety of the mountains. But he was soon starved into surrender when Edward's ships cut off corn supplies from Anglesey. The King treated Llewellyn fairly. Once he had paid homage he was left in control of Gwynedd, but he had to give up his other lands.

There matters might have rested, but for Llewellyn's brother David. Complaining at the harsh treatment of his countrymen by English officials, David rebelled in the spring of 1282. Llewellyn joined him, reluctantly, and all Wales rose in revolt. The King now decided to crush the troublesome Welsh once and for all. Again Llewellyn was surrounded by the English in his mountain stronghold. This time he broke free and escaped southwards, but he was killed in a skirmish at Orewin Bridge, near Builth, in December 1282.

Llewellyn's head was sent in triumph to London and fixed on a spear above the Tower. Six months later David was captured and executed. By then Welsh resistance had already collapsed. Edward took control of Snowdonia and divided it into counties, like the rest of his kingdom. The marcher lords were given lands in Wales, which was now wholly under English law and government. The Welsh were no longer free, but to this day they have kept alive their old Celtic language and many traditional customs.

Beaumaris Castle on the Isle of Anglesey. It was begun in 1295, after a Welsh revolt the previous year. No less than 400 stonemasons were employed in constructing it. Notice the outer ring wall completely surrounds the defences inside. Nowadays the inner ward is marked out with tennis courts!

Castles among the conquered

To strengthen his hold on Wales, Edward built castles round the fringes of Snowdonia. Without delay the work of construction began at Conway, Caernarvon and Harlech. A further castle, at Beaumaris on Anglesey, was started a few years later. All four were situated near the coast, so their garrisons of English soldiers could receive supplies by sea if the Welsh rose in revolt.

Edward had built other castles in Wales earlier in his reign (see map). But they could not compare with the mighty fortresses round Snowdonia, which are among the finest of the whole Middle Ages. Instead of having a single square keep, like earlier stone castles, Edward's architects planned *concentric* defences (one circle of walls inside another). The most important rooms led into a central quadrangle, or *inner ward*. Beyond this, between the two rings of walls, was the narrow *outer ward*. Here any attackers who got past the main gate would find themselves caught between two showers of arrows.

The towers built into the walls were important for defence. In the old square keeps it was impossible for archers to shoot at attackers close underneath the walls without exposing themselves to returning fire. But in these later castles towers curving outwards made it easy for defenders inside to shoot along the faces of the walls.

Edward I's great Welsh castles still stand today as monuments to his reign. It was at Caernarvon that his son, the future Edward II, was born in 1284—most probably in temporary royal quarters on the site of the present castle. When the young Edward was seventeen his father gave him the title Prince of Wales. Ever since then kings' eldest sons have received the same honour.

Llewellyn's death almost marks the end of the long struggle between the Welsh and the English—but not quite. A century later, in 1400, a powerful Welsh landowner, Owen Glendower, led his people in a last bid for freedom. Many castles of King Henry IV and his marcher lords were captured by the rebels, and a number of English armies were defeated. At the height of his power Owen controlled nearly the whole of Wales. But after several years of bloodshed and destruction the fires of revolt flickered out. Owen disappeared and died in an unknown hiding place.

'The Hammer of the Scots'

Unlike Wales, Scotland had its own line of kings. They ruled over a country which fell into two distinct halves. In the rolling hills and lowlands south of the Firth of Forth there lived many families of English and Norman descent. Here land was shared out among feudal lords and the way of life was similar to that in England. But the wild Highlanders of the North were much more like the Welsh — wandering herdsmen with their own language and customs. They disliked the English and even looked on the Scottish Lowlanders as foreigners, as indeed many of them were.

It was an unexpected turn of events that allowed Edward I to extend his power north of the Border. At the beginning of his reign Scotland was peaceful, prosperous and united under a strong king,

The castle and town walls of Conway (darkened in this photograph to make them stand out). The whole circuit is 1400 yards round, with three gates and twenty-one towers. Inside the castle is a suite of rooms designed for the King during his visits to Wales

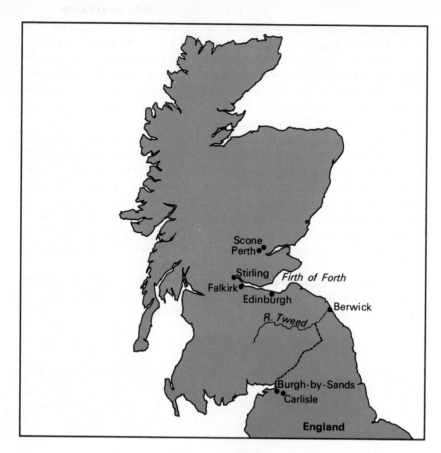

Scotland in the reign of Edward I

The coronation chair in Westminster Abbey. Enclosed beneath the seat is the 'Stone of Destiny' that Edward I took from Scone in 1296

Alexander III. But one stormy night in March 1286 disaster struck. Alexander was thrown from his horse while riding alone along the northern shore of the Firth of Forth, and when his companions found him next morning he was dead.

Unfortunately for Scotland Alexander left no son to follow him. His daughter, who had married the King of Norway, was dead, but she left a baby girl named Margaret who was then just three years old. So Alexander's little granddaughter, the 'Maid of Norway', was proclaimed queen. Four years later she set out for Scotland. But the Maid became very ill on the voyage and had to be landed in the Orkney Islands, where she died.

The throne was vacant, and no less than thirteen Scottish nobles claimed it—all distant relatives of the dead King. There was a risk of civil war breaking out, so Edward I was invited to help decide between the rival claimants. It was a perfect opportunity for him to increase his influence in Scotland. After several meetings with lawyers and leading nobles, he chose John Balliol, Lord of Galloway, to be King (1292). The decision was fair, but Edward insisted that John must do homage to him as his overlord.

It soon became clear that John Balliol was a 'puppet king', controlled by his powerful overlord. The Scots hated this English interference and finally forced John to go against Edward's wishes.

Edward's answer was to gather an army, march into Scotland and force Balliol to give up the throne (1296). The English King now considered himself master of Scotland. Before returning home with Balliol as his prisoner, Edward aimed to show the Scots that they would never have another king of their own. He went to the abbey of Scone, near Perth, and took away the block of stone on which Scottish kings had been crowned.

But lasting peace between England and Scotland was not to be achieved by force. As soon as Edward turned his back the Scots rose in rebellion, led by a humble knight named William Wallace. Many Scottish nobles were unwilling to join the rebellion, because they had estates on both sides of the Border and did not want to offend Edward. But the ordinary farmers and clansmen had no doubts about which side they were on. Armed with axes and long spears, they crushed an English army at Stirling (September 1297) and drove its commander, the Earl of Surrey, from their land.

In the following spring Edward marched north to teach the Scots the lesson he had taught the Welsh. His army contained a strong force of archers armed with *longbows*. These deadly weapons, five or six feet high, could fire iron-tipped arrows through chain-mail! Edward's archers quickly settled the issue at the battle of Falkirk (1298). Wallace fled into hiding and the rebellion was broken. Edward, 'the Hammer of the Scots', now ruled Scotland through a council of nobles. By 1304 the last great castle—Stirling—fell into English hands. And in the following year Wallace was captured, after seven years on the run. He was taken to London and hanged.

Stirling Castle today. Most of the medieval buildings have been replaced, but the picture shows the excellent defensive position of the castle, known as 'the Gateway to the Highlands'

Effigy of Edward II, from his tomb in Gloucester Cathedral. Although athletic and courageous, he was not the warrior king that the English nobles looked for. He preferred music, rowing and play-acting to fighting. He was finally deposed and murdered by his own nobles in 1327

The marble tomb of Edward I in Westminster Abbey. A motto on the side reads: EDWARDUS PRIMUS SCOTTORUM MALLEUS HIC EST: PACTUM SERVA (Here is Edward I, the Hammer of the Scots: keep thy faith). In 1774 the tomb was opened. The embalmed body measured 6 feet 2 inches—an enormous size for a man of the thirteenth century

Robert Bruce fights back

The Scottish struggle for freedom seemed lost. But it only needed a spark to fire the smouldering discontent of the people. This was provided by Robert Bruce, grandson of one of the thirteen who had claimed the throne after the Maid of Norway's death. Bruce gained the support of a group of nobles and got himself crowned King of Scotland in March 1306.

It seemed unlikely that Bruce's reign would last long. All the chief Scottish castles were in English hands. Within a year he had lost two battles and could only wander, homeless and outlawed, in the western Highlands. Meanwhile Edward I, now old and feeble, travelled north with a powerful army. But the strain was too much for him and he died in July 1307 at Burgh-by-Sands, near Carlisle. He left orders that his bones should be carried at the head of the advancing army. But his son, now King Edward II, lacked his father's fighting spirit. He called off the invasion and returned to bury his father's body in Westminster Abbey.

Just before the old King's death the tide turned for Bruce. Supporters flocked to his side and he began to win battles and skirmishes against the English. In later years men told a story of how he had been ready to give up the struggle as he sat one day in a cave, watching a spider try to make its web. After many falls it finally succeeded and Bruce gained fresh heart. The story may well have been invented, but Bruce's recovery was real enough. One by one he captured the English-held castles, until after seven years Stirling, the greatest of them all, was at his mercy.

Edward II could not let Stirling fall without a fight. In June 1314 he crossed the Border with about 20,000 men. Bruce's army was outnumbered by about three to one; but it was well placed, on a wooded ridge above a stream called the Bannock Burn, just south of Stirling. The two armies met on Midsummer's Day, the Scots attacking downhill and taking the enemy by surprise. The fighting was long and bitter, but the swift-moving Scots were better led and more confident. After suffering heavy losses the English fled in disorder.

The battle of Bannockburn was the greatest blow ever struck for Scottish freedom. In 1328 a new English king, Edward III, finally made

Statue of Robert Bruce
(1274–1329) at Stirling
Castle

peace with Bruce and accepted him as the rightful ruler of Scotland. Edward I's plan to unite the English and Scottish crowns had to wait another 300 years, until 1603, when James VI of Scotland became James I of a United Kingdom. In the meantime, both countries went on quarrelling and fighting. Raiders from both sides of the Border stole cattle and caused much death and destruction.

More about Wales and Scotland

For details about soldiers, weapons and armour see Chapter 19.

Books

M. McCririck, *Stories of Wales, Book 1* (E. J. Arnold).

G. Williams, *Owen Glendower* (O.U.P., Clarendon Biographies). Only for advanced readers.

M. E. Reeves, *The Medieval Castle* (Longman, Then and There series). Last chapter.

W. K. Ritchie, *Scotland in the Time of Wallace and Bruce* (Longman, Then and There series).

W. C. Dickinson, *Robert Bruce* (Nelson, Picture Biographies).

D. Scott-Daniell, *Battles and Battlefields* (Batsford). Chapter 4 for the battle of Bannockburn.

W. K. Ritchie, *Scotland and the Normans* (Longman, Then and There series).

Filmstrips

Edward I (Rank, *Reign by Reign* series).

Ciné Film

Castles in Cambria (E. A. Meaden, Leicester).

Visits

The great castles of 'Snowdonia': Conway, Caernarvon, Beaumaris, Harlech.

Edward I's tomb in Westminster Abbey.

Stirling Castle.

To write and find out

1 Make a timescale of the period 1270–1330, based mainly on events in Wales and Scotland. Draw a six-inch line down the left hand side of the page and mark it off on a scale 1 inch = 10 years. First mark the reign of Edward I, perhaps with a coloured line. Then fill in the main events described in Chapter 16 and in any other books you have read.

2 The Romans invaded Wales and Scotland in the first century A.D. Compare their campaigns with those of Edward I. How were the results similar? Why do you think Scotland was so hard to conquer?

3 Among the long-established customs kept alive by the Welsh people perhaps the best known is the *Eisteddfod*, a yearly congress of bards and musicians. When did it start? What happens at an *Eisteddfod* nowadays?

17 Town Life and Trade

Nowadays people living in Britain's largest towns may go for weeks or even months without seeing a cow, a ploughed field, or farmland of any sort. Street after street of houses, factories, office blocks and shops cut off the modern town dweller from the world outside. But in the Middle Ages most towns were no bigger than large villages today, so their inhabitants were never far from the sights and sounds of the countryside. Pigs and poultry wandered among the houses. Cattle and sheep were driven through the streets. Open fields, pastures and meadows surrounded the town and supplied much of its food.

Most medieval town dwellers spent some time working on the land, even in large cities such as London, Bristol, Norwich and York. London, the centre of government, had a population of about 40,000 in the fourteenth century and was more than twice the size of any other town in the British Isles. Yet sittings of its law court were stopped at harvest time, and craftsmen were expected to leave their workshops and help 'cut, gather and bring in the corn'. Wealthy Londoners kept hawks and hounds and went hunting in the neighbouring woods and open spaces.

Drawing of the walled medieval city of Salisbury. As towns grew, in the later Middle Ages, houses were built beyond the protecting walls

Weavers' cottages at Lavenham in Suffolk. Notice that the upper storeys of some were built out to overhang the street. This gave passers-by some protection from the rubbish thrown out of the top windows. In very narrow streets neighbours on opposite sides could reach out of their windows and almost touch one another!

Walls, streets and houses

Medieval towns were centres of trade; places to which people came to buy and sell. In those days traders needed extra protection for their money and goods. So stout defences were built round towns— usually stone walls—to keep out robbers and vagabonds. At Chester, York and several other places large parts of the old walls can still be seen. They had strong gates, guarded by gatekeepers who opened them at dawn and shut them at sunset. Any stranger noticed entering a town was closely questioned about his business.

Inside the walls the streets were narrow. A few might be surfaced with cobble stones, but most were just earthy tracks. In dry weather carts, horses and people on foot stirred up clouds of dust. However, when it rained heavily streets became seas of mud. There were no proper drains and no dustmen to collect rubbish. Each citizen was supposed to keep the street clean in front of his house, but instead most people dumped their garbage and slops there!

Buckets and chamber pots were emptied out of windows. Passers-by ran for cover when they heard the familiar cry of 'gardey loo!' (slang for *gardez l'eau*, meaning 'look out, water!'). Channels ran down the middle of most streets and these became open sewers, flowing into the nearest river. In London the Thames, which took most of the City's sewage, also provided much of its drinking water. Not surprisingly, diseases spread rapidly in these conditions, especially among children who played around the rotting garbage.

The closely packed huts of the poor were little different from those of village peasants. They had thatched roofs and windows covered with wooden shutters or oiled linen, which let in some light. All the family slept in one room, on straw mattresses. The houses of crafts-

153

Shoemakers at work. Notice the customer being served at the front of the shop, while men make shoes inside

men were larger, with two or even three floors. They were built on a strong framework of timber and had white plaster walls.

A craftsman's house normally had a shop on the ground floor. It did not have a glass window at the front. Goods were displayed on stalls or benches facing the street. Inside was the workroom, where customers could see the goods being made. The shopkeeper and his family lived above the shop, in private rooms reached by a flight of steps outside. Down some streets all the shops were of the same kind. In London, tailors lived in Threadneedle Street, bakers in Bread Street, fishmongers in Fish Street and so on.

Street names helped strangers to find their way about the town. Other useful landmarks were the taverns, or ale-houses, with their gaily painted signs. Taverns did not stay open all evening like pubs today. At sunset, when the town gates were closed, bells rang—warning all citizens to go home. The unlit streets were dangerous

places at night, when they became the haunts of thieves and murderers. In Bristol any keeper of a tavern who failed to close his doors on hearing the bell was fined two shillings (equivalent to several pounds today).

Wooden buildings were in constant danger of catching fire, and where they were close together the flames spread quickly. Buckets of water were little use once a fire had taken hold. The people tried to pull down the walls and thatched roofs of neighbouring houses to check the spread of the flames. Ropes and long fire-hooks were kept handy for this purpose. In London it was ordered that stone walls must be built between wooden houses. These helped to keep fires under control, as did the growing number of tiled roofs.

Even the most crowded towns had some breathing spaces. There were often allotments or vegetable gardens inside the walls, and places where livestock might be pastured after sunset, when they were brought in from the fields. The houses of the rich were usually spaced out by gardens, orchards and stables. Noblemen and a few wealthy merchants could afford to build in stone. The finest of these town mansions had tiled floors, brick fire-places, oak-panelled walls and glass windows well in advance of most country manor houses.

Churches were also built of stone. Medieval towns had an amazingly large number of them, many with fine towers or pointed spires. Norwich had fifty churches and London well over 100 in the later Middle Ages. On Sundays citizens in large towns must have been almost deafened by the ringing of church bells!

Borough charters

To begin with many towns were on royal estates and were thus under the direct rule of the king. Others were controlled by the local baron, bishop or abbot who held the land on which they were built. This meant townsmen had to work and do other services for their lord, just like village peasants. But as towns grew and prospered their citizens preferred to concentrate on making and selling goods. So they tried to strike a bargain with the king or lord which would free them from labour services in return for a sum of money and a fixed yearly rent.

Where such agreements were made the details were set out in a charter. The town gained the title of *borough* and its citizens were called burgesses. Each burgess was a free-man, renting his own *burgage* or plot of land in the town. He was also entitled to farm strips in the town fields and sell his goods in the market without paying the fees, or *tolls,* that were charged to outsiders.

Royal charters were sold to a large number of towns by Richard I and John, two kings who were always short of money. John alone granted more than seventy in seventeen years. Towns with a charter from a local lord normally tried to purchase one from the king as well, giving much wider privileges. These included the right to govern themselves by electing a mayor and council of aldermen, who had power to make by-laws for the town and collect taxes. Royal charters also allowed boroughs to have their own law court and a merchant guild.

A carved oak chest, which was probably used for storing clothes, documents or valuables, and also for sitting on. Even the wealthiest families had little furniture. The master of the house might have a proper chair, but the rest of the family sat on stools and benches. The prized possession was often a four-poster bed, with a feather mattress and curtains all round to keep out draughts

The guildhall at Thaxted in Essex

Merchant and craft guilds

In most boroughs the leading merchants formed themselves into an association called a guild. Its aims were to encourage trade and also to control it, for the benefit of members, by making all visiting merchants pay tolls on goods they sold in the town. Such guilds grew rich and powerful. They built fine guildhalls, which were often rented to town councils for their meetings. If the town was a port the merchant guild might own part of the waterfront.

London had no merchant guild, but each group of craftsmen—weavers, goldsmiths, carpenters, hatters and the rest—formed separate craft guilds. In time most other English towns had craft guilds too. Each guild made strict rules to control the quality and price of the goods its members made and sold. If any member was found to be making shoddy goods, using false coins or faulty weights and measures he was heavily fined.

A craft guild was not like a modern trade union. The employers, called masters, belonged to it as well as those who worked for wages. In fact, the masters controlled the affairs of their guild. It was they

Stonemasons and carpenters in the thirteenth century working together on a building

Right: A guild master judges the work of a stonemason and carpenter. One drills a piece of wood, while the other shapes stone with a hammer and chisel

Journeymen and apprentices

who bought the materials and sold the finished products. And masters trained all new recruits, called apprentices, in 'the art and mystery' of the craft. An apprentice lived in his master's house and agreed to work for him for a fixed number of years, usually seven. He was not paid wages, but he was fed, clothed and given a straw bed in the shop downstairs.

When a young man finished his apprenticeship he became a journeyman, working for daily wages (the word comes from the French *journée*, meaning day). A journeyman was free to work for any master, in any town. If he wanted to become a master himself he had to prove his skill by producing a 'masterpiece' of his work. Guild officials judged whether it was up to the required standard. If he passed the test, the journeyman still had to make a large payment to the guild before he was accepted as a master. Many highly skilled craftsmen never had enough money for this, so they remained journeymen all their lives.

Every guildsman paid a yearly subscription into his guild's 'common box'. This money was used to help members who had fallen on bad times through illness, accident or old age. When a member died his funeral was paid for and his widow given a pension. Some of the larger guilds founded their own schools, chapels and almshouses for the poor or aged.

Guilds did not forget pleasure and entertainment. Each had special feast days when members walked in a colourful procession wearing their special dress, or *livery*. After a church service they enjoyed a great banquet. At one such banquet in Salisbury the guildsmen ate 10 lambs, 2 calves, 16 pigs, 70 chickens and 100 pigeons! Guilds also presented 'miracle plays' in which they acted Bible stories. The stage was usually a decorated wagon called a *pageant*, which was drawn round the streets. Angels went up to heaven on ladders, God had a beard and wicked kings wore turbans! A whole set or 'cycle' of plays was performed over several days, one by each guild.

Stalls in a cobbled market place. What is each trader selling? The goods were sold by the gross and dozen, as today, and by pounds, bushels and *ells* (a measure of 45 inches, for cloth). In the market place the town crier sometimes made his public announcements, after ringing his bell to attract attention

The Lord Chancellor's Woolsack in the House of Lords

Markets and fairs

Every town had at least one weekly market, when stalls were set up in an open space near its centre. Countryfolk walked or drove their carts in from the surrounding villages, bringing eggs, butter, cheese, livestock and perhaps fruit to sell to the townspeople. In return they purchased cloth, shoes, salt, pots, pans and other iron goods. Markets were also attended by travelling pedlars, who brought knives, mirrors and all sorts of trinkets such as pins, buckles and ribbons.

These regular markets satisfied the ordinary day-to-day needs of local inhabitants. But some people occasionally wanted to buy and sell rarer, more expensive articles. So in certain towns and on the estates of a few lords great fairs were held, usually once a year. To have a fair, a town council or lord required the 'licence and goodwill' of the king. This royal permission had to be paid for, and the king also received a toll on all dealings.

Most fairs were held on feast days of saints, although they carried on for a week or more. Famous ones included St Bartholomew's in London, St Giles's at Winchester and Stourbridge Fair, outside Cambridge. Besides local tradesmen and farmers, merchants came from all over the kingdom and from overseas. Wealthy ladies could buy fine silk for their dresses, jewels, perfume and other costly luxuries. Gentlemen bought weapons, hawks for hunting, horses, leather saddles and harnesses. They also stocked up with French wine, candles, pepper and other spices used to improve the taste of salted meat.

Poor folk, unable to buy such expensive goods, still walked miles to a fair because it was a place for merry-making as well as buying and selling. There were jugglers, acrobats, dancing bears, puppet shows, wrestling matches and other attractions. Cook shops selling hot meals did a busy trade, and so did taverns. Ale was cheap and many people got drunk.

There are so many shops nowadays that fairs are no longer necessary for trading. But they continue in a number of places, purely for entertainment. Nottingham Goose Fair, which began in the Middle Ages, is still held each autumn. However, today people go not to buy geese or other animals but for the roundabouts, coconut shies, rifle ranges and so on.

Wool—England's wealth

In the middle of the House of Lords, at Westminster, there is a large red object looking like a sofa without arms. It is stuffed with English wool, and the Lord Chancellor, the chairman of the House, sits on it. This custom of sitting on the 'Woolsack', as it is called, goes back to the Middle Ages. It reminds us that wool was once the basis of England's wealth.

In medieval times English wool was the finest in Europe. Large quantities were sold to cloth workers on the Continent, especially after the sheep-farming Cistercian monks arrived in England in the twelfth century. Merchants travelled around the hills and dales of Yorkshire, Gloucestershire, Somerset and other areas where sheep flourished, buying up thousands of fleeces. Some of the wool was used in England. The rest was carried to the ports on packhorses and exported to the chief cloth-making areas of Flanders (now Belgium) and North Italy.

Some of the fine cloth made in Flanders from English wool was exported to England. Thus profits from wool sales were used to buy back the finished product. This was not good business for England, and some kings tried to encourage the growth of a home industry. Edward III made laws to stop exports of wool; and weavers, dyers and other craftsmen from Flanders were invited to settle in England, where they passed on their skills. Gradually the English began to make not just coarse material for ordinary use but also cloth fit for lords and kings. A prosperous industry grew up around towns such as Stamford, Lincoln, Norwich and Colchester.

Many processes were needed to turn a dirty, tangled fleece into a fine piece of cloth. The wool had to be washed and combed or 'carded' to disentangle the fibres. Then it was spun into tightly twisted yarn. This was usually done with a distaff and spindle (see picture) although spinning wheels were also used in the later Middle Ages. Spinning was young women's work—hence the term 'spinster' for one who is unmarried. Next the yarn was woven into cloth on a loom, worked by hand and foot. It could be dyed either before or after weaving.

There now followed a most important process called fulling. The cloth was beaten in water to shrink and thicken it and give it a felted look. This could be done with clubs or with feet and hands, and 'fuller's earth' was added to the water (a white, powdery substance dug out of the ground). From the twelfth century, fulling mills were introduced—simple water-mills which turned wooden hammers attached to a revolving drum. These speeded up fulling and made it more effective. Finally, the cloth was stretched out to dry and its surface brushed and levelled with a pair of shears.

As a rule each group of craftsmen worked at home, in their own workshops. A merchant 'clothier' bought the wool and passed it on from one group of craftsmen to the next. He paid them for their work and then sold the finished product himself. We call this 'domestic industry', in contrast to modern factory industry in which workers are gathered in one place.

By the fifteenth century English cloth-makers were outpacing their rivals in Flanders and Italy. The main centre of the industry was now in the Cotswold Hills, where fast flowing streams drove the fulling mills. All over Europe high prices were paid for 'broadcloths' from Castle Combe, Stroud, Bradford-on-Avon, Cirencester, Malmesbury and other thriving villages and small towns. Instead of being exported, England's wool was used by its own craftsmen. Before long the Kingdom became as famous for finished cloth as it had once been for raw wool.

Trade over the seas

At this moment vast quantities of goods are being shipped to and from England safely and speedily. But in the Middle Ages sea trade

Packhorses carrying woolpacks. Most merchants used packhorses because few roads were fit for carts or wagons. For several months of the year thick mud and deep ruts made many roads and tracks impassable. Merchants normally travelled in groups, as a protection against robbers and outlaws

'Spinsters' at work. The girl in the middle uses the things like hair brushes to 'card' or disentangle the wool. The one on the left holds a *distaff* under her arm (a stick with prongs to hold the mass of wool). The yarn is drawn out and twisted by a *spindle* (a kind of heavy spinning top)

A woman weaving on a hand-loom. This was usually men's work. To make the best broadcloth a wider 'broadloom' was used, which needed two men to work it.

Dyers at work. Notice the bundle of sticks, used to feed the fire under the vat. Common dyes, such as woad (blue and black), madder (red) and weld (yellow) were made from plants grown in England. But others, including saffron (a yellow made from crocuses) and scarlet (made from an insect found in the Mediterranean lands) had to be imported

The Hanseatic League

was slow, difficult and dangerous. Maps were unreliable, pirates thick along many coasts and the ships themselves unsafe in rough seas. The merchants of northern Europe carried their cargoes in short, blunt-ended sailing vessels called *cogs*. These had rudders at the stern, like modern ships, but few had more than one mast and their square sails made progress against the wind very difficult.

Most trade between England and the Continent was controlled by powerful groups or companies of foreign merchants. The largest of these—the *Hanseatic League*—was formed in the twelfth century by trading towns near the Baltic and North Sea coasts. Hanse merchants, mostly Germans, set up a base in London with the permission of Henry III. Their ships brought salted fish, timber, dyestuffs, furs, pitch and iron goods. In return they bought English goods for re-sale on the Continent. Apart from London other east coast ports, including Newcastle, Hull and King's Lynn, profited from trading with the Hanse merchants.

Model of a fifteenth century *cog*. Sailors today would not think such ships fit for more than coastal trading. But in medieval times they battled across the Baltic and North Seas. There were no warships in northern Europe, so merchant vessels had to be used in sea battles. Hence the 'castles' at each end, used by archers. We still call a raised deck at the front of a ship the *fo'c'sle* (forecastle)

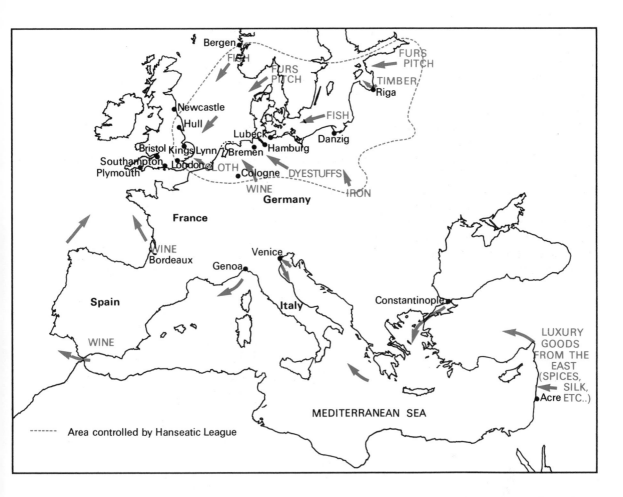

The following labels appear on the map:

Bergen
FISH
FURS PITCH
FURS PITCH
TIMBER
Riga
Newcastle
Hull
Lubeck
FISH
Bristol Kings Lynn
Danzig
Hamburg
Southampton
Bremen
CLOTH
Plymouth
London
Cologne
DYESTUFFS
WINE
IRON
Germany

France

WINE
Bordeaux
Genoa
Venice

Spain
Italy
Constantinople

WINE
LUXURY GOODS FROM THE EAST (SPICES, SILK, Acre ETC..)

MEDITERRANEAN SEA

------ Area controlled by Hanseatic League

English imports in the later Middle Ages

The Hanseatic League controlled most of the trade of northern Europe. Similarly, Italian merchants from the great cities of Venice and Genoa dominated trade with the Mediterranean lands and the countries of the East. Their long, graceful galleys were frequent visitors to Bristol, Plymouth, Southampton and especially London. Italians brought mainly luxury goods for the rich—silks and other rare fabrics, carpets, jewels, ivory, gold, perfume, glassware, Mediterranean fruits and wines, and above all spices such as pepper, ginger, nutmeg and cloves.

The Italian merchants, skilled at banking and book-keeping, became the most powerful group of foreign traders in London. To this day the chief banking district in the City is Lombard Street (named after the Lombards of North Italy). Londoners were jealous of their wealth and blamed them for every misfortune that befell the City. Occasionally there were riots against foreigners—not only Italians but also Hanse merchants, Flemings (from Flanders) and French traders who brought casks of wine from Gascony.

To pay for imports, the English exported mainly food and raw materials—wool, corn, hides, cheese, tin from Cornwall and lead from Derbyshire. But in the later Middle Ages the growth of industries, especially cloth-making, meant manufactured goods could be sold too. Besides woollen cloth, England exported fine leather goods, and cups, mugs and plates made from pewter (a mixture of lead and tin). English merchants also began to take a hand in the export trade. Groups of *Merchant Adventurers* were formed in the main ports, with the aim of founding trading centres abroad, as their rivals had done in England. The Merchant Adventurers were to play a great part in the future growth of English trade.

More about towns and trade

Books

M. E. Reeves, *The Medieval Town* (Longman, Then and There series).

D. Birt and J. Nichol, *The Development of the Medieval Town* (Longman History Games).

K. Durwent, *Medieval London* (C.U.P., Discovering London, no. 3).

A. F. Titterton, *A Port and a Pilgrim* (Ginn's History Bookshelves, Green Shelf). Pages 1–21.

The Merchant Adventurers (Cape, History Jackdaw series, no. 45).

Filmstrips

The Medieval World (Longman, Then and There Filmstrips). No. 3: Town life; home life, travel.

The Medieval Town, and Medieval London, Parts 1 and 2 (Educational Productions Ltd.).

The Town (Common Ground, Medieval Life).

Ciné film

Life in a Medieval Town (Gateway Educational Films Ltd).

Visit

One of the woollen cloth towns or villages mentioned in this chapter or other books on the subject. What evidence can you find of the medieval industry? (Look for churches or stone houses built by rich merchants, names of public houses, streets and so on.)

To write and find out

1 Make a list of the things done today in building a house which were not done in the Middle Ages.

2 If you live in a town look carefully at the street names in its oldest quarter. Write down those based on medieval trades or crafts. Has the town got a charter? If so, when was it granted and by whom?

3 Many English surnames are based on medieval trades—for example, smith, baker, carpenter, fuller, draper, weaver, taylor, brewer, tanner, glover, bowman, fletcher (arrow maker), tiler, barber, saddler, butcher, dyer and spicer.
   (a) Make a list of people you know with these or similar names.
   (b) Make a list of modern trades that do *not* go back to the Middle Ages.

Dress in the later Middle Ages

A PEASANT and his wife. Both wear simple tunics with shoes and belts of leather. Underneath, the wife wears a petticoat of linen or wool; her husband has woollen stockings which he rolls down in warm weather. Medieval clothes had no pockets, so pouches were necessary for carrying money and other small belongings

A NOBLEMAN and his wife. Over his close fitting doublet the noble wears a gown trimmed with fur. Shoes with long pointed toes were fashionable then. His wife's gown is called a *houppelander* and is made of silk. By law, only men and women of noble rank were allowed to wear the finest cloth and most costly furs. But these *Sumptuary Laws* were often broken by rich merchants and their wives, who liked to show off their wealth by dressing like nobles

18   Black Death and Peasants' Revolt

During the spring and summer of 1348 Englishmen lived in fear of a mysterious and unseen enemy. Merchants, seamen and travellers talked of a terrible plague that was spreading across Europe. It first appeared in the seaports of Sicily and Italy the previous autumn. In a few months hundreds of thousands of men, women and children had died in Italy, Spain and France. With each new outbreak the plague moved nearer the British Isles.

The great plague

All over England people knelt in prayer or made pilgrimages to ask for deliverance. But while ships still crossed the Channel there was little chance of the Kingdom escaping infection. August came, and with it the dreaded plague—first reported in Dorset. Large swellings, some as big as apples, appeared under people's armpits and between their legs. These were quickly followed by black and blue blotches all over the body. Some people vomited and spat blood, their breath turning foul and stinking. Very few recovered from it. Within three days of being infected most sufferers were dead.

The 'Black Death', as some called it, was probably what modern doctors know as the *bubonic plague*. Even today it is a danger in parts of Asia. It is carried by fleas on the black rat (not the common brown rat, familiar in England) and can be passed on by the slightest contact with an infected person. The Black Death was first reported in China in 1334. So it probably reached Italy by means of rats on merchant ships carrying goods from the East.

The cause of the plague was discovered less than 100 years ago, so people in the fourteenth century had no idea how to prevent its spread. They knew nothing about germs and the link between dirt and

Above: Procession of monks in 1349 praying

Ingarsby, in Leicestershire, was one of the many villages abandoned about the time of the Black Death. Hardly anything can be seen of it from the ground, but the places where houses once stood show up in this aerial photograph

for deliverance from the Black Death

Left: Medicines being prepared. Many different kinds of herbs were used, along with less pleasant ingredients such as the insides of dead animals

disease. Some tried drinking vinegar, avoiding moist foods or bleeding themselves. Such 'remedies' seem ridiculous to us, but in the Middle Ages medical science was almost non-existent. Most people calling themselves doctors depended on guesswork and superstition. Patients were given medicines containing anything from crushed rocks to insects.

No part of England escaped the plague entirely, and it soon spread to the rest of the British Isles. Dead bodies littered fields and roads all over the countryside. But the worst outbreaks were probably in the towns, where more people came into close contact. In London and other large towns cemeteries were quickly filled and fresh burial grounds had to be found. Deep trenches were dug and cartloads of corpses shovelled into them. Men were paid high wages for this work, because most people were afraid to go near plague victims.

By the end of 1350 the plague died down in England. Some writers of the time said it had killed half the people. But the figure was probably nearer a third — or well over one million people out of a total population of almost four million. The Black Death returned frequently in the years ahead. Many who lived through the first terrible outbreak were struck down when it re-appeared in 1356, 1361–2 and 1368–9. But in time people must have developed some resistance to it, because most later outbreaks were mild in comparison with that of 1348.

Troubled times

The Black Death left its mark on England long after its victims had been buried in the ground. In some places whole villages were abandoned for lack of men to sow and reap the crops. Grass grew on the lanes and pathways, and deserted cottages fell into ruin. Lands once covered with carpets of corn were left to sprout weeds.

Before the Black Death, going as far back as the twelfth century, many villeins had been freed from their labour services to the lord of the manor. Instead of having to work part of the time on the lord's land they paid him rent for their cottage and strips. With this money the lord hired free labourers to work for wages. Most lords found that wage labourers worked harder than villeins who were always anxious to get back to their own strips.

After the plague, however, workers were scarce. Labourers realised

167

their increased value and demanded more wages than before. Many lords paid up, rather than let their crops rot for lack of hands to gather them in. The same happened in the towns. Masters had to pay higher wages to get enough journeymen to work for them.

Parliament tried to put a stop to these demands. Laws were made ordering that wages should remain as they had been before the plague. Men who travelled in search of higher wages were to be branded on the forehead with a red hot iron! At the same time Parliament asked for more and more taxes to pay for unsuccessful wars in France. Angrily, working men ignored the laws and tried to avoid the taxes.

Meanwhile, those who were still villeins saw the increased advantages of being free-men, now that wages were rising. So they tried to exchange their labour services for money rents. Some lords agreed, but others refused to give villeins their freedom. They strictly enforced all labour services, and made sure that slackers were fined in the manor court. Villeins became bitter and restless. The adventurous ones gathered their few possessions and fled, with their wives and children. They could easily find work in a town or on another manor. Men were so hard to get that good wages were paid to newcomers and no questions asked about where they came from.

The common people of England, seeing the chance to better themselves, grew discontented with their lords and masters. There were threats of violence against some lords, including a number of abbots and bishops who refused to free their villeins. Because their estates belonged to the Church, many abbots and bishops claimed they should not rent them out or interfere with the old customs in any way. Villeins no longer accepted such excuses. They had lost respect for wealthy, pleasure-loving Church lords. So had many poor priests, who were firmly on the side of the peasants.

The march to London

In the counties round London a travelling priest named John Ball stirred up the people against their lords. He attacked the greed of nobles and merchants and the idleness of many Church leaders. Ball said that things would not go well in England until there were no more lords to live off the sweat of the common people. In village after village men remembered his words:

'When Adam dalf [dug the ground] and Eve span,
Who was thanne the gentilman?'

Banned from preaching in churches, Ball went into the streets and market places, attracting large crowds. 'We are men formed in Christ's likeness,' he said, 'and they treat us like beasts.'

John Ball did more than preach. He and a group of determined followers plotted a rising of the common people. The seeds of revolt were beginning to grow when, in 1377, Richard II, a boy of ten, came to the throne. For a time the kingdom would have to be ruled by a council of nobles, most of them unpopular. Protests and gatherings of peasants and tradesmen were reported in several areas in 1377, 1378 and 1379.

Trouble came to a head when Parliament, meeting in November

Richard II (1377–99). His father, Edward the 'Black Prince', was a great warrior. But Richard grew up to love books, music and art—not the sorts of interests that barons looked for in a king. After a troubled reign he ended up losing his throne and being murdered in a castle dungeon at the age of 33

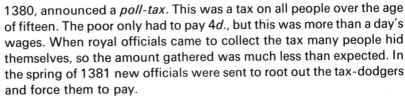

1380, announced a *poll-tax*. This was a tax on all people over the age of fifteen. The poor only had to pay 4*d*., but this was more than a day's wages. When royal officials came to collect the tax many people hid themselves, so the amount gathered was much less than expected. In the spring of 1381 new officials were sent to root out the tax-dodgers and force them to pay.

In parts of Essex and Kent crowds drove away the tax-collectors and the 'Peasants' Revolt' had begun. In fact it was more than a revolt of peasants. Many tradesmen, parish priests, friars and outlaws joined in. On both sides of the Thames men took down scythes and sickles, sharpened axes and knives, or cleaned the swords and longbows they had fought with in France. Early in June the leaders met, at Maidstone in Kent, and chose a man named Wat Tyler to be their captain.

The rebels aimed to march to London and put their demands before the King, now aged fourteen. They had no quarrel with Richard himself. In fact they thought of him as their true leader. It was the council of nobles, the unpopular lords, tax-gatherers, lawyers and Church leaders who were in danger. As the armies from Essex and Kent swarmed towards London they attacked a number of manor houses and destroyed documents giving details of villeins' labour services. Prisoners were freed from jails—among them John Ball, whom the Archbishop of Canterbury had imprisoned at Maidstone.

By the evening of Wednesday, 12 June the Essex men had camped in the fields of Mile End, just outside London. The men of Kent camped on Blackheath, five miles from London Bridge. We can only guess at their numbers, but there were probably at least 60,000 on both sides of the Thames. The King and his advisers took refuge in the Tower. Troops were on guard there, but they were not used. The rebel army was much too large to be crushed by force.

Wat Tyler meets the King

The rebel leaders sent word to Richard that they wished to speak with him. So next day the King and his advisers were rowed down the Thames towards Blackheath. But when the royal attendants saw the rebel forces face-to-face they refused to let the King land. The royal barges stopped and moved slowly away, amid shouts and insults from those lining the river bank.

Tyler and the other leaders now decided to enter the City. No fighting was necessary. The common people of London opened the gates and welcomed the rebels. Across London Bridge streamed the men from Kent and other southern counties. Meanwhile the Essex men, with supporters from Hertfordshire, Suffolk and Cambridgeshire, marched in from the east, through Aldgate.

There were strict orders against looting and destruction. But first a few scores had to be settled. The prison in Fleet Street was broken open, the hated lawyers of the Temple were attacked, and the magnificent Savoy Palace, home of the King's uncle, John of Gaunt, was destroyed. Luckily for Gaunt he was out of London at the time, so the rebels had to be content with ransacking and burning his palace. From the Tower, Richard and his nobles saw the flames light up the night sky. The King would have to meet the rebels before it was too late.

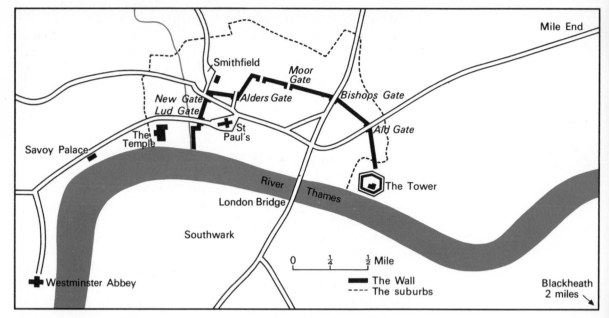

Early next morning, Friday 14 June, Richard left the Tower with an escort of nobles and soldiers. As the jostling crowds struggled to catch a glimpse of him, he rode to Mile End, where Wat Tyler was waiting. Tyler came slowly forward on his pony, dismounted and kissed the royal hand. Then he put forward the peasants' demands, which included the abolition of feudal services, the renting of land at 4d. an acre, and the deaths of all 'traitors' to the people. Richard granted these requests, but added that only a court of law could decide whether a man was a traitor.

The peasants wanted proof of Richard's promises to take back to their lords. So thirty clerks set to work writing charters of freedom. Meanwhile, a band of rebels burst into the Tower. Inside they found Simon Sudbury, Archbishop of Canterbury, and royal ministers who had been responsible for the poll-tax. They were all dragged to Tower Hill and beheaded. More executions of 'traitors' followed—mostly lawyers, tax-collectors and foreign merchants.

Once they had their charters many peasants went home. But the leaders stayed in London, still with a strong army, and another meeting with the King was arranged. This took place in the evening at Smithfield, a market and fair-ground. Again Tyler rode up on his pony and greeted Richard warmly. He demanded that lords' estates should be reduced to 'narrow proportions' and the lands of the Church should be divided among the people. Once more Richard agreed.

It was a hot day and Tyler called for a mug of water. He rinsed his mouth and spat on the ground. This may have seemed bad manners in front of a king, but by the standards of the time it was not unusual. As he mounted his pony, one of the King's followers shouted at him and a scuffle broke out. William Walworth, the Mayor of London, wounded Tyler, and a young squire finished him off. We shall never know whether it was Tyler's behaviour which caused the fight, or whether the royal attendants had planned to kill him.

When the rebels realised what had happened they drew back their bows. The royal party was in danger of being massacred, but Richard saved them. Spurring his horse towards the peasant ranks he called out: 'Sirs, will you shoot your King? I am your captain, follow me.' Bewildered, but still trusting Richard, the people followed him into the open farmlands to the north. There he repeated his promises and talked them into going home. It was a triumphant moment for the young King.

Work for the hangman

Once the rebels were safely dispersed, the King and his council broke all the promises made at Mile End and Smithfield. Soldiers were gathered and any peasants left in London were arrested. Every house-holder in the City had to swear his loyalty to the King's government on a Bible. The next step was to put down the rising in the countryside and root out the ringleaders.

Royal forces went first into Essex, accompanied by the King and his judges. Everywhere the charters granted to villeins proved not to be worth the parchment they were written on. At Waltham the King told a gathering of peasants: 'Villeins you were, and villeins you shall remain.' His forces moved through the county, putting down scattered attempts at resistance. In Chelmsford and Colchester batches of rebel leaders were sentenced to death and hanged. In Kent too the roadside gallows soon creaked under the weight of rotting bodies.

In one form or another the rising spread as far north as York and as far west as Devon. But the main risings were in the south-eastern counties. The town of St Albans in Hertfordshire was on the estate of an abbey, and its citizens had long been refused the right to control their own affairs. On June 15 they ran riot, draining the abbot's fish-

The trouble spots in south-eastern England, 1381

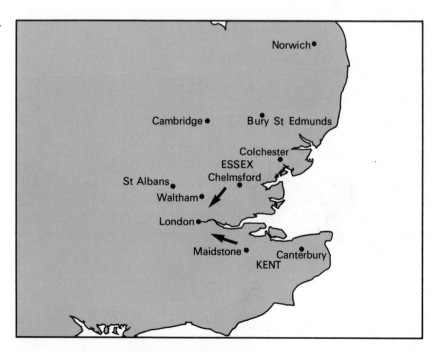

The death of John Ball

pond, killing the game in his woods and dividing his estate among themselves.

The abbot was forced to sign a borough charter, but soon afterwards a royal army arrived and the rebel leaders were rounded up and hanged. With them died John Ball. He had been captured in the Midlands and taken to St Albans for trial. Openly admitting his part in the revolt he went bravely to the gallows in the early morning light of July 15.

Bury St Edmunds, in Suffolk, was another town on the estates of an abbey, and the rising of 1381 was not the first in its unhappy history. Knowing the townsmen and peasants were after his blood, the abbot fled. But he was hunted down and killed in a wood some miles away.

Left: A fifteenth-century picture showing the execution of the Archbishop of Canterbury on Tower Hill. As he kneels (bottom left) his bishop's hat, or *mitre*, falls to the ground. This was later nailed to his skull when his head was stuck on London Bridge. The two who died with him were the King's Treasurer, Sir Robert Hales, and John Legge, organiser of the poll-tax

Top: John Ball, whose ideas did so much to start the Revolt

Bottom right: The dramatic events at Smithfield. This fifteenth-century picture combines two incidents in one. On the left Tyler is attacked by the Mayor, while Richard watches; on the right the King (looking much older than fourteen) rides towards the rebel ranks. The peasants are shown to be much better equipped than they really were. Some had bits of armour, but most were in smocks and jerkins

A gallows. All over southeast England in the summer and autumn of 1381 tattered figures swung from gallows like this

His head was paraded round the town, together with that of the King's Chief Justice, Sir John Cavendish.

In the neighbouring county of Norfolk, the gates of Norwich were opened to a large rebel band. Peasants and tradesmen took over the castle and made knights wait on them at table! Not far away, at Cambridge, the people beheaded a judge and burned Corpus Christi, a college of the University, which owned much property in the town. But here, as in other towns and villages, the rejoicing of the people was short-lived. Troops arrived and before long there was more work for hangmen.

By the autumn the revolt had been completely crushed. On the surface it seemed the peasants had failed. But a rising as large and as well organised as that of 1381 was bound to leave its mark. Within ten years all attempts by Parliament to keep down wages were abandoned. And within fifty years nearly every lord had given up trying to force unwilling villeins to give labour services.

More about the Black Death and Peasants' Revolt
See Chapter 20 on the ending of labour services.

Books
The Black Death (Cape, History Jackdaw series, no. 50).
The Peasants' Revolt (Cape, History Jackdaw series, no. 36).
J. Lindsay, *Nine Days' Wonder* (Dobson). The story of Wat Tyler.
D. M. Stuart, *London Through the Ages* (Methuen). The section dealing with the Peasants' Revolt.
M. Price, *The Peasants' Revolt* (Longman, Then and There series).
D. Turner, *The Black Death* (Longman, Then and There series).

Filmstrips
Social Life in Medieval Times (Visual Information Service). The final frames are on the Peasants' Revolt.
Richard II (Rank, *Reign by Reign* series).

To Write
1 Describe the Peasants' Revolt from the point of view of an Essex or Kent man who marched to London and was present at Wat Tyler's death.
2 'Wat Tyler let victory slip from his fingers.' If you had been the Peasants' leader, in complete control of London and the government, what would you have done to make sure Richard's promises were kept? (Why do you think such schemes did not occur to Wat Tyler?)
3 *(a)* Find out why Richard II, after such a triumphant start to his reign, ended up being murdered by his own nobles.
   (b) Find out who discovered the cause of the bubonic plague, in the nineteenth century. In which countries is it still a threat today?

19 The Hundred Years War

The kings of England had ruled lands on both sides of the Channel since the Norman Conquest of 1066. By the time of Henry II, in the twelfth century, the English Crown controlled more than half of France. But the French kings aimed to drive out their English rivals. Nearly all the lands Henry ruled were soon lost—most of them in the reign of his son, the unfortunate John.

When Edward III became king of England, in 1337, only the south-western provinces of Gascony and Guienne remained in English hands. These were important wine producing areas. Every year thousands of casks of French wine were shipped from Bordeaux to London, Bristol and Southampton. English merchants and nobles feared that this flourishing trade might be spoilt if the French king conquered Gascony and Guienne. They urged Edward III to fight to keep these territories.

Edward needed no encouragement. He enjoyed fighting and looked forward to wars in France. His mother was a French princess and he claimed he had more right to the French throne than King Philip VI (1328–50). Philip was a cousin of the previous king, but Edward was a nephew. The French nobles did not want Edward as their ruler, and he must have realised he had little chance of getting the crown of France. But if he was successful in battle at least Gascony and Guienne would be safe, and he might gain other lands too.

After lengthy arguments between the two kings, Edward declared war in 1337. It was the start of a long series of raids and English invasions, with intervals of peace in between, which lasted until 1453. We call it the 'Hundred Years War', although the actual fighting amounted to much less than 100 years.

Edward III's army
Feudal armies of mounted knights had gone out of fashion by this time. Like his grandfather, Edward I, the King used large numbers of archers and other foot-soldiers, as well as knights on horseback. Each of the nobles commanding the royal forces made an agreement with the King to recruit a certain number of men, some mounted and some on foot.

Every soldier received wages from the royal treasury. Knights got 2 shillings a day, archers with horses 6d., unmounted archers 3d. and peasant foot-soldiers 2d. The commanders were also paid—earls 6s. 8d. a day, and ordinary barons 4 shillings. Allowing for changes in the value of money, this was a better paid army than those which fought in the World Wars of the twentieth century.

Archers used the longbow—the weapon Edward I had found so deadly in his Scottish wars. They wore iron caps, stout leather jackets, and sometimes a short sword hung from their belts as well as a quiver

Effigy of Edward III (1327–77) in Westminster Abbey. He was the kind of warrior king that nobles respected and were keen to follow into battle. He loved the excitement of war and the glory of victory. Although he fought against the King of France, Edward was himself half French by birth and spoke French more easily than English

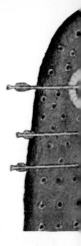

English longbowmen practising. The targets, banked up with mounds of earth, were called *butts*.

The badge of the present-day Grand National Archery Society, showing a longbowman of about the year 1400. Notice he had a metal breastplate buckled over his jerkin. His longbow, made of springy yew, elm or hazelwood, had a tough string of hemp or linen. Arrows were tipped with iron and feathered with quills from geese, turkeys or swans

of arrows. Longbowmen were not found among the poorer peasants. They were freemen; usually either town tradesmen or small farmers who rented their own land. It took great skill to shoot a longbow accurately, so regular practice was essential. Edward III encouraged this. In 1369 he ordered the citizens of London to give their spare time to archery, *not* ' . . . the throwing of stones, wood, iron, hand-ball, foot-ball . . . nor such other like vain plays, which have no profit in them'.

Edward's knights, carrying shields and lances or swords, were much more heavily armoured than those of earlier centuries. Over their coats of mail, most knights now wore specially shaped pieces of plate armour to give extra protection to the chest, knees, elbows, feet and other parts of the body. Hands were covered with iron gauntlets, and the helmet protected the whole head, with a *visor* (small hinged cover) over the face.

A full set of plate armour was so heavy that if a knight was knocked off his horse he was barely able to defend himself. He might be killed or captured if there was no one near to help him escape. Over his armour a knight wore a linen tunic, or surcoat, with his family's coat-of-arms embroidered on it. This was the only sure way of recognising him on the battlefield.

To get an army across the Channel, complete with horses, siege towers, and all the equipment of cooks, blacksmiths and other necessary tradesmen, Edward needed a large fleet of ships. He could afford to keep only a few ships of his own. The rest were hired from merchants. The so called 'Cinque Ports' of Dover, Romney, Sandwich, Hastings and Hythe, had a special duty to provide the Crown with ships. Dozens more came from towns all along the coasts of England.

Longbows at Crecy
The first big battle of the war took place at sea, near the port of Sluys in Flanders (1340). An English fleet of 200 ships, loaded with soldiers, was about to land when a much larger French fleet was sighted. The English, with the wind and tide in their favour, attacked immediately. Many French ships were at anchor, so their crews were easy targets for English longbowmen shooting from the raised 'castle' decks. Some enemy vessels were held with iron 'grappling hooks'

while soldiers boarded them and fought hand-to-hand. At the end of the day the French fleet was almost entirely destroyed.

The victory at Sluys gave Edward control of the Channel. His kingdom was safe from invasion, yet he could attack the French at any time. English raids in the next few years caused terrible destruction in France. Armies 'lived off the land', seizing the crops and cattle of helpless peasants. The homes of the rich were plundered and burned, and costly tapestries, goblets, candlesticks and other valuables were carried back to England. Captured French nobles were held to ransom for large sums of money.

The English armies fought short summer campaigns, retreating quickly to the coast before King Philip could gather his forces. However, in August 1346, after a raid in Normandy, Edward was caught up by a large French army and forced to give battle at Crecy. The English numbered about 12,000 but the French King had twice as many men. Edward realised his best chance was to select a good defensive position and let the enemy do the attacking.

English troops embarking for France during the Hundred Years War. Notice the royal coats-of-arms. They combine the lions of England with the French royal badge—the lilies, or *fleurs-de-lys.* Edward III changed his coat-of-arms to this design when he claimed the French throne

The siege of Calais

Philip's archers, most of them Italians, used cross-bows. These fired iron-tipped bolts, which fitted into a groove and were released by a trigger. But they took some time to re-load and could not shoot as far as longbows. Before the enemy cross-bows could get within range the English archers, firing six times a minute, scattered them with showers of arrows. Then the French knights charged. But arrows 'as thick as snow' brought horses and men crashing to the ground. Hundreds of knights were trampled to death or suffocated in their armour. As darkness fell the English moved forward and the surviving French fled from the battlefield.

Knowledge of gunpowder had just reached England from the East, and Edward is said to have used cannon at Crecy. But this can hardly have affected the result of the battle. The earliest cannon often burst and were a greater danger to the gunners than to the enemy! Not for another two or three hundred years would the use of gunpowder lead to entirely new methods of warfare.

After Crecy, Edward marched north and attacked the port of Calais. He met strong resistance and had to carry on a siege right through the winter before the starving citizens surrendered. Calais was the home of many pirates who plundered English shipping in the Channel. These were driven out and settlers from England took control of the town. Calais became a base for English merchants and a useful stronghold on French soil.

France during the Hundred Years War

A later painting of the battle of Crecy, 1346. The French King's cross-bowmen are retreating (bottom left). One of them is loading his bow by turning a *windlass*. There were several other ways of reloading a cross-bow, but all wasted valuable time in the midst of a battle

Edward returned home in triumph. At this stage the war was popular among his subjects and he tried to keep up their interest in fighting. Many 'tournaments' were arranged, where fully-armed knights showed their skill in *jousting* (mock battles on horseback with blunted lances). Spectators came from miles around and cheered as lances splintered and knights were hurled from their saddles. Jousting was never more popular in England than at the time of Edward III's French victories.

English ups and downs

English raids into France continued, some led by the King's warlike son Edward, known as 'the Black Prince'. He was described by a writer of the time as 'courageous and cruel as a lion'. After one expedition, in 1356, the Prince, with about 7,000 men, was cut off by a

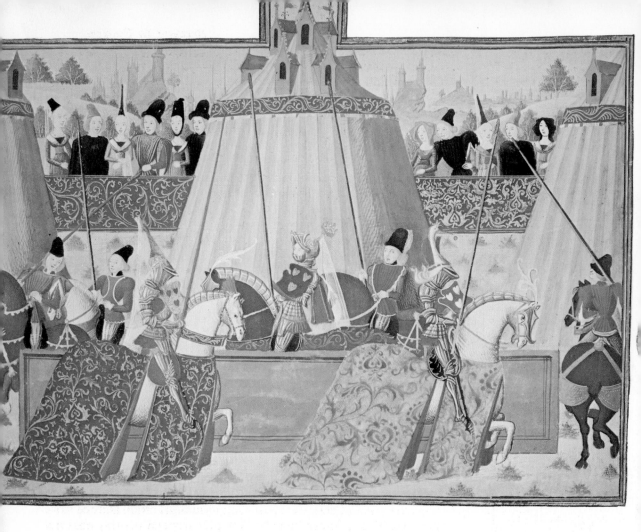

French army of 15,000 at Poitiers (pronounced *Pwotty-ay*). The French King, John II (who succeeded his father Philip in 1350) was determined to crush the Prince.

However, the French seemed to have learned nothing from their defeat at Crecy. They still relied on cross-bows and the old-fashioned charge of heavily armed knights. The English longbowmen, given good cover by hedgerows, brought down the opposing knights in such numbers that piles of dead horses and helpless riders blocked the advance of their own foot-soldiers. The battle dragged on for three days, until finally the English knights attacked the enemy in the rear and forced them to retreat. King John was captured and taken to England, where he was held to ransom.

A break in the fighting came in 1360, when the rival kings made peace (Treaty of Bretigny). Edward gave up his claim to the French throne, and in return he kept Calais and a large area round it. Also his lands in south-western France were greatly increased. Edward's success was surprising, against a kingdom with a population three or four times the size of England's. The smaller English armies had tried to avoid full-scale battles. Yet when forced to fight, at Crecy and Poitiers, they demolished the enemy!

Knights jousting at a tournament. The contestants aimed to unhorse each other by charging down opposite sides of a wooden barrier, which prevented the horses from colliding. Grandstands were put up for the spectators, and ladies gave scarves, or *favours*, to their favourite knights

An effigy of the Black Prince from Canterbury Cathedral. Compare the armour shown here with that of the knights pictured in Chapters 10 and 13

The war re-started in 1369 and English fortunes soon changed. The French at last found a skilful commander in Bertrand du Guesclin. Although only a humble knight from Brittany, Bertrand rose to become Constable of France, in charge of the royal army. He concentrated on defence, ordering castles and town walls to be strengthened. The raiding English were kept at bay until they ran short of supplies and had to return home. Meanwhile the French, with many new ships, began to challenge the English control of the Channel. Damaging attacks were made on coastal towns in Kent and Sussex.

King Edward was growing old, and the Black Prince, his best general, fell ill and was soon unable to fight. Little by little the French recovered their lost territories. When Edward died (1377) his lands in France had been reduced to a few coastal towns, including Calais and Bordeaux, and the districts surrounding them. The war was now unpopular in England and there were frequent protests at the heavy taxes collected to pay for it. Richard II finally made peace in 1396.

Henry V and Agincourt

Not until 1413 did England have a king who was willing and able to renew the war in France. He was Henry V—young, ambitious and every inch a soldier. Henry claimed to be the rightful king of France, as Edward III had done, and made speedy preparations for war.

There was great disorder in France. King Charles VI (1380–1422) suffered from fits of madness and could not control his nobles, who quarrelled fiercely. Taking advantage of this unrest, Henry landed in Normandy (1415) with 8,000 men. After a five-week siege he captured the port of Harfleur. But a serious illness called dysentery reduced his army to about 6,000. Henry marched north to Calais, planning to return home and collect fresh troops.

On the way to Calais Henry was surprised by a French army of more than 20,000 and forced to fight in thickly wooded country near the castle of Agincourt. It was late in October and there had been heavy rain. Henry positioned his men in a gap between two woods and ordered his archers to stick sharp wooden stakes in the ground in front of them.

Two groups of knights attacked the wings of the English army and

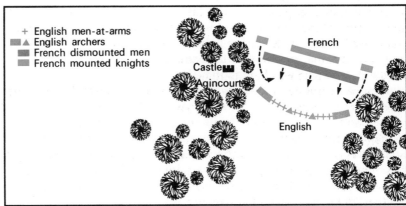

Plan of the Battle of Agincourt

the main French force of foot-soldiers advanced down the centre. The knights were driven back by the deadly English arrows before they reached the enemy lines. Meanwhile the French foot-soldiers found their heavy chain-mail a great handicap as they struggled across sodden plough-land. The gap between the woods narrowed as the French came forward, with the result that soldiers were crammed together like sardines. A French nobleman who fought at Agincourt later wrote: 'Before they could come to close quarters, many of the French were disabled and wounded by the arrows; and when they came quite up to the English, they were . . . so closely pressed one against another that none of them could lift their arms to strike.'

Many Frenchmen sank up to their thighs in the mud. The lightly clad English archers saw their chance. Throwing their bows to the ground they ran forward and fell upon the enemy with swords and knives. The battle was won. At least 7,000 dead and dying Frenchmen lay on the battlefield, while English losses amounted to only a few hundred!

Henry went home to a hero's welcome. But he was soon back across the Channel, and within five years he had conquered all northern France. The French nobles were still quarrelling, and one of them, the powerful Duke of Burgundy, went over to Henry's side. In 1420 the French queen made peace, allowing Henry to keep the lands he had conquered (Treaty of Troyes). It was also agreed that the English King would marry her only daughter, Catherine, and take over the French crown when her insane husband, Charles VI, died.

Henry V (1413–22). When he came to the throne he was twenty-six; tall, strong and energetic. He impressed everyone by his kingly manner. Like Richard I, Henry won great victories in war but achieved little of lasting value to his kingdom

The tide turns—Joan of Arc

Henry V never achieved his ambition of becoming King of France. He died in 1422, a few months before the wretched Charles VI. But even if he had lived longer Henry would not have got the French throne without a fight. Charles had a son—also called Charles, but known as the *Dauphin* (eldest son). The Treaty of Troyes had ignored the Dauphin's claim to the throne. Yet most Frenchmen considered him their rightful ruler. They certainly did not want Henry's son, Henry VI, who succeeded to the English throne at the age of eight months!

The war was far from being over. The Duke of Bedford, brother of Henry V, now began the difficult task of forcing France to accept the infant King. He was a skilful general and soon proved more than a match for the Dauphin. Pale, thin and rather feeble, Charles just wanted to be left alone in his palace. In 1428 the English began a siege of Orleans, aiming to attack the south of France, which still supported the Dauphin (although he had not been crowned). Charles was on the point of despair when one day a sixteen-year-old girl arrived at his court saying she could save France!

Her name was Jeanne d'Arc (Joan of Arc) and she came from a peasant family in Domrémy, on the eastern borders of France. Joan spent most days looking after her father's sheep on the hillsides near her home. She said that for some time she had been hearing heavenly voices, and St Michael, St Catherine and St Margaret had appeared, each telling her that she had been chosen to save her country from the English. After a while Joan asked an army captain to send her to the Dauphin. He laughed at first, but she seemed so earnest and sincere that in the end he agreed.

Joan had an unexpected message for Charles: 'The King of Heaven bids me tell you that you shall be crowned in the cathedral at Rheims' (the city where French kings were usually crowned). The Dauphin's courtiers giggled and Charles himself thought Joan very strange. But she seemed so confident that he accepted her help. Joan put on armour and rode off with an army to Orleans, which was still being besieged.

Soon after Joan's arrival the English were defeated and driven from the walls of Orleans (1429). This proved to be the real turning

Statue of Joan of Arc
at Rheims

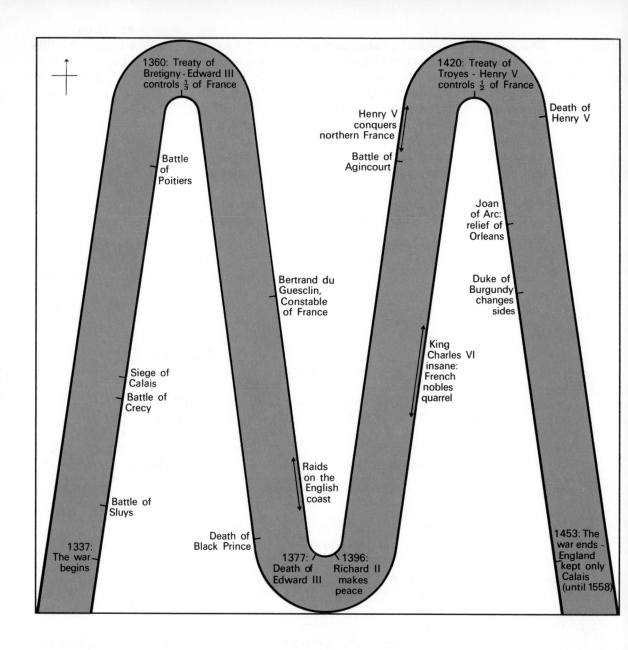

1360: Treaty of Bretigny - Edward III controls ⅓ of France

1420: Treaty of Troyes - Henry V controls ½ of France

Henry V conquers northern France

Death of Henry V

Battle of Poitiers

Battle of Agincourt

Joan of Arc: relief of Orleans

Bertrand du Guesclin, Constable of France

Duke of Burgundy changes sides

King Charles VI insane: French nobles quarrel

Siege of Calais

Battle of Crecy

Raids on the English coast

Battle of Sluys

Death of Black Prince

1337: The war begins

1377: Death of Edward III

1396: Richard II makes peace

1453: The war ends - England kept only Calais (until 1558)

point in the war. 'The Maid of Orleans' now led the Dauphin to Rheims, where he was crowned Charles VII, just as she had promised.

Joan's triumphant career as a soldier soon came to an end. In 1430 she was captured and sold to the English by their ally, the Duke of Burgundy. She was accused of being a witch, possessed of evil powers, and after a long trial she was condemned to death by a French church court. In May 1431 Joan, still only nineteen, was burnt at the stake in the market place at Rouen. Years afterwards the Church's view of her changed and she was made a saint.

Joan's death could not save the English from defeat. After his coronation Charles seemed to find new strength and powers of leadership. One by one, cities and castles were recaptured, and in 1435 the

The rise and fall of English fortunes in the Hundred Years War

Duke of Burgundy went over to the French side. The English position was now hopeless. By 1453 they had been driven out of the whole of France (except Calais, which remained under the English Crown until 1558). The Hundred Years War was over, and French kings were at last to be masters in their own country.

More about medieval armies and the French wars

Books

R. R. Sellman, *Medieval English Warfare* (Methuen's Outlines series).

M. Blakeway, *An Archer in the Army of Edward III* (O.U.P., People of the Past).

E. K. Milliken, *Archery in the Middle Ages* (Macmillan, Sources of History series). Only for advanced readers.

P. Nicolle, *A Book of Armour* (Puffin Picture Book).

R. H. and S. Wilmott, *Discovering Heraldry* (U.L.P.).

R. J. Mitchell, *The Medieval Tournament* (Longman, Then and There series).

The Battle of Agincourt (Cape, History Jackdaw series, no. 32).

Joan of Arc (Cape, History Jackdaw series, no. 10).

E. Kyle, *Maid of Orleans* (Nelson, Picture Biographies).

J. Williams, *Joan of Arc* (A Cassell Caravel Book). For reference.

Ivanhoe, a novel by Sir Walter Scott. Chapter 8 for a description of a tournament.

Filmstrips

The Hundred Years War (Hulton).

The Hundred Years War (Gaumont British Educational Films).

The Colour of Chivalry (Educational Productions Ltd.).

Joan of Arc (Visual Publications).

Henry V (Rank, *Reign by Reign* series).

Visit

Armoury of the Tower of London—for knights' armour, longbow and early cannon.

To write

1 If you had been in command of the French army at Agincourt, what different tactics would you have used to take advantage of your superiority in numbers? Illustrate with your own battle plan.

2 *(a)* Do you think it would have been a good thing for England if its kings had gained, and kept, the crown of France?

   (b) Imagine how life might be different today if Britain and France were joined in one kingdom.

3 Why do you think Joan of Arc was condemned as a witch? What reasons could the Church have given for its verdict?

20   A Time of Change

Defeat in the Hundred Years War meant English kings ruled an island kingdom, for the first time since 1066. Across the Channel only Calais belonged to England, and even that small foothold on the Continent was given up a century later. As a result of losing the French lands Englishmen began to feel a stronger sense of belonging to one nation, with its own customs and with clearly defined boundaries, mostly set by the sea.

When Edward III began the long war, back in 1337, he did not think of it as a contest between 'Englishmen' and 'foreigners'. He was half French himself, and so close were his ties with France that he claimed to be its rightful ruler. To Edward the war was mainly a personal rivalry between himself and the King of France. And the soldiers on both sides fought for glory and personal gain, including plunder and ransom money, not because they loved their countries.

To men of Edward's day Europeans were divided into nobles, gentlemen and peasants rather than English, French or Italians. But by the later stages of the war such views were beginning to change. Joan of Arc spoke of 'saving France', and a French chronicler wrote:

In the opinion of many, the English are not human beings and men, but senseless and ferocious beasts, which go about devouring people.

Such hatred of the 'foreigner' was a sign of growing national pride among the peoples of Europe.

King Henry IV (1399–1413) was the first King of England after 1066 to speak English as his native language

Chaucer, Caxton and 'our englysshe langage'

In medieval England nobles, churchmen and peasants were divided not only by wealth and upbringing but also by three different languages. Latin was written and spoken by scholars and men of the Church. Most books were in Latin, and its grammar was the basis of all education. After the Norman Conquest French-speaking kings and lords ruled England, and only the peasants and tradesmen of Saxon stock spoke English.

However, even among common folk there was not one English tongue but many, for there were dozens of *dialects* (varieties of the same language). Strong traces of these remain today, but in the Middle Ages it was often impossible for people from different parts of the country to understand each other.

French died out very slowly in England. It was not until Edward III's reign (1327–77) that English became the chief language of the royal court and of Parliament. By then many French words, and Latin ones too, had blended with the Old English. It was a richer language, usually offering a choice of words with similar meanings. For example, today Old English words such as great, small and begin have French-based alternatives: grand, petty and commence.

William Caxton, 1422–91

A well-known figure in Edward III's court was the poet Geoffrey Chaucer (see Chapter 15). His *Canterbury Tales* and other works were written in English. They were greatly admired and other poets tried to copy Chaucer's style and use of words. Consequently the form of English spoken by Chaucer and the people of London gradually came to be understood by educated men in other parts of the country. It was an important step towards a common English language.

Copies of Chaucer's poems, handwritten on parchment, were hard to come by and very expensive—as were all books in the Middle Ages. But this was soon to change, because in the middle of the fifteenth century a printing press was invented in Germany. John Gutenberg, a citizen of Mainz, is thought to have produced the first printed book, soon after 1450. Previously men had only been able to 'block print' pictures carved on wood. But the German press had movable type, so pages of writing could be set up. The craft of paper-making had recently come to Europe from the East, and this, together with printing, made books a lot cheaper.

Knowledge of printing was brought to England by William Caxton, a wealthy English merchant who lived for many years in Bruges, a town in the Netherlands. Caxton enjoyed collecting books and spent much of his spare time translating French works into English, carefully copying them out himself. When he heard about the invention of printing in Germany he went there to study the new craft. Later he constructed a press in Bruges, where in 1475 he printed the first books in English.

Caxton brought his press to London in the following year and set up a workshop near the Palace of Westminster. In the remaining fifteen years of his life he printed copies of nearly 100 different books. Most were in 'our englysshe langage', and the *Canterbury Tales* was among them. Caxton's publications were clear and easy to read, but they took much longer to print than books nowadays. The type had to be assembled and inked by hand.

Like Chaucer, Caxton used the form of English known in the London area. 'Certaynly it is harde to playse euery man', he wrote, because 'englysshe that is spoken in one shyre varyeth from another.' However, Caxton's books, together with the works of Chaucer and his imitators, did much to fix a single form of written English. As education spread, this became the language of all the people.

John Wycliffe and the Lollards

From the time of Chaucer to Caxton there was growing criticism of the Church. It had an enormous income from estates covering a third of the kingdom. But much of this wealth was not put to good use. Many bishops, monks and friars were more interested in earthly pleasures than the good of men's souls.

The humble parish priest in Chaucer's *Canterbury Tales* is a sincere and religious man. This was probably true of most poor priests. But Chaucer's begging friar, who '. . . knew the tavernes wel in every toun', and his wealthy monk, whose greatest joy was hunting the hare, were also drawn from real life. Chaucer made fun of such

German printing press

Gret chere made our oſt to vs euerychon
And to ſouper ſett he vs anon
He ſerued vs wyth vytaylle at the beſte
Stronge was the wyne & wel drynke vs lyſte
A ſemely man our oſte was wyth alle
Forto be a marchal in a lordes halle
A large man he was wyth eyen ſtepe
A fayrer burgeys is ther non in chepe
Bolde of hys ſpeche and wel was y taught
And of manhood lacked he right nought
Eke therto was he right a mery man
And after ſouper to pleyen he began
And ſpak of myrthe amonge other thynges
Whan that we hadde made our rekenynges
He ſayd thus now lordynges truely
Ye be to me right welcome hertly
For by my trowthe yf I ſhal not lye
I ſaw not thys yeer ſo mery a companye

t iiij

Part of the Prologue to *The Canterbury Tales,* taken from one of the earliest printed editions, 1485

Below: In 1377 Wycliffe (left) was made to answer for his views before Simon Sudbury, the Archbishop of Canterbury who was murdered in the Peasants' Revolt four years later. The meeting took place in St Paul's Cathedral, but, as this later painting shows, it was broken up by fighting. Wycliffe had become involved in a quarrel between a group of powerful nobles and the bishops. This probably saved him from serious punishment

pleasure-seeking churchmen, but others of his day thought it no laughing matter. One was John Wycliffe (1320–84), a scholar and teacher at Oxford University. His attack on the medieval Church was to shake its whole foundations.

Lands and possessions had no place in God's Church, said Wycliffe. He urged monks and bishops to give up all their worldly riches and lead simple lives, as the early friars had tried to do. Wycliffe believed that Christians should not obey any churchman who went against Christ's teachings and lived in luxury. Men who lacked grace had no right to preach the Word of God, he said.

Above all, Wycliffe wanted the Bible translated from Latin into English. Then more people could read it for themselves and would not have to rely on what priests saw fit to tell them. But the leaders of the Church were opposed to the idea of ordinary people having the Bible in their own tongue. They claimed that only churchmen

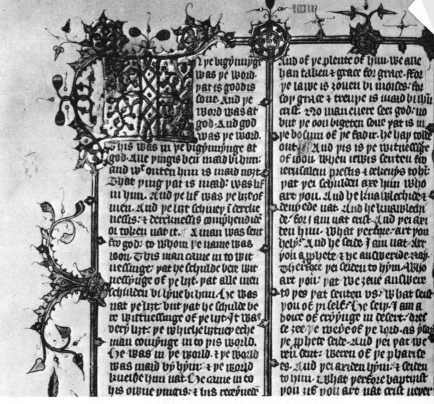

An extract from Wycliffe's
English Bible

Lollards being led to execution

could understand its true meaning, and it was their task to explain it to the people. Wycliffe thought this was nonsense. Without asking permission he and some of his Oxford friends set out to translate the Bible themselves.

The first complete English Bible was finished in 1382. In the same year Wycliffe was expelled from Oxford on the orders of the bishops. Not content with disobeying them and criticising their way of life, he had questioned some of their teachings. He said they had no reason for believing that the bread and wine on the altar changed into the real body and blood of Christ during the service of the mass. He also said that there was no need for a pope, because Christ was the only Head of the Church.

John Wycliffe died peacefully in 1384. But his attack on the Church was not forgotten. Forty-five years later his body was dug up, burnt to ashes and thrown in a river! By then his views were widely known in England and on the Continent. A number of 'Poor Preachers', mostly humble priests who had studied under Wycliffe, made it their business to spread his ideas. They held gatherings of ordinary people in the towns and villages, and read from the English Bible. Their enemies called them 'Lollards' (babblers or mumblers) but their preaching found strong support among common folk.

The bishops were determined to silence the critics of the Church. Many Lollards were arrested, tried before church courts and imprisoned. Some who refused to confess the error of their ways were burnt at the stake. These executions forced Lollards to go into hiding. But Wycliffe's ideas were kept alive, especially by groups of town tradesmen. Bristol, Reading and Coventry were among the strongest centres of 'Lollardy' in the fifteenth century.

The Church could not go on silencing its opponents for ever. In many parts of Europe large numbers of Christians had become dissatisfied with their religious leaders. By the sixteenth century a few kings and princes had joined the growing ranks of *Protestants* (the name given to those who protested). Several rulers, including Henry VIII of England, broke away from Rome and set up churches in their own countries. Monasteries were closed and their lands taken away. These religious changes or reforms, known as the *Reformation,* are described in the third book in this series: *The Early Modern Age.*

Rents instead of services

The people of medieval Europe were brought up to serve two lords— one in heaven and one on earth. Their duties to the heavenly Lord were laid down by the Church; and their duties to an earthly lord were governed by 'feudal' customs and rules (services in return for land). Religious beliefs, and services to the lord of the manor, were the foundations of medieval life. But feudal customs began to decline even before the power of the Roman Church.

At first the chief purpose of feudal lordship was to provide the king with an army of knights. But as early as the reign of Henry II (1154–89) the King's tenants were beginning to pay money (scutage) instead of doing military service. The King used this money to hire soldiers in France. Before long the whole army was paid wages, and alongside mounted knights marched archers and other foot-soldiers drawn from the common people.

A similar changeover from services to money payments gradually took place in the towns and villages. Townsmen purchased charters from their lords or from the king giving them control of their own

In the fifteenth century there was a great increase in sheep farming in England. What products from sheep do you think the women on the right are carrying?

Sheep farming

affairs (Chapter 17). Likewise, in the countryside, lords of the manor began to allow villeins to pay rent instead of working for them. This change was already well under way before the Black Death speeded it up (Chapter 18).

In some European countries there were unfree peasants 'tied to the soil' as late as the nineteenth century. But in England most villeins had bought their freedom from labour services by the fifteenth century. Some sold their strips in the fields and made a living working on other men's land for wages. Others saved up enough money to buy or rent extra land. In time they became fairly prosperous 'yeomen farmers', employing more and more wage-labourers to work for them.

The end of labour services on the manor did not mean the end of 'open field' farming. Free peasants still cultivated scattered strips and grazed livestock on common pastures. However, in some places lords turned plough-land over to pasture, enclosed it with hedges and kept sheep. The growth of the woollen cloth industry made sheep farming very profitable.

There were many more sheep than people in fifteenth century England. The fall in population due to outbreaks of the plague had not yet been made up. After reaching a peak of nearly four million before the Black Death in 1348, the population of England and Wales was below three million a century later.

The Middle Ages and today

Of course people did not get up one morning hundreds of years ago and say: 'That's the end of the Middle Ages. Now for the Early Modern Age'! All historical periods were invented long afterwards by scholars who saw some shape or pattern in the past. Such periods are a useful framework for studying history, but they are very blurred at the edges. In other words, it would be wrong to say that the Middle Ages ended, or began, on an exact date.

History never stands still. Changes have taken place continuously ever since our distant ancestors made the first stone tools. However, at certain times the pace of change has quickened. For Europeans, one such time was the century between about 1450 and 1550. It saw the end of a single Christian Church and, in England at least, the other great 'prop' of medieval life—feudal lordship—fell away too. These years also saw the first printing presses and the growing importance of gunpowder. Hand guns as well as cannon were in use by the time of Caxton. Before long, knights in armour, archers and castles were to be as out-dated as handwritten parchment books.

In 1453, while the Hundred Years War was ending in France, a dramatic event took place on the other side of the Continent. The great city of Constantinople was besieged and finally captured by

Fifteenth century hand gun

The coronation of
Elizabeth II in 1953.
Many parts of the
ceremony date from the
Middle Ages

Muslim Turks. The thousand year-old Byzantine Empire was no more. Some of its finest scholars had already fled to Italy, where their knowledge helped to bring new ways of life and thought in the West. Thus the fall of Constantinople was both an end and a beginning. It is the starting point of the next book in this series.

The scholars of Constantinople had preserved the learning of ancient Greece. In a similar way, people today keep alive medieval customs and beliefs, often without realising it. All over Europe men and women worship in medieval churches and cathedrals, while the Catholic Church is still the largest of all the Christian communities. Most people live in towns and villages that were settled and named in the Middle Ages. Even the names of the people themselves often remind us of medieval trades and occupations.

In Britain we still have kings and queens, and they are crowned at Westminster in much the same way as William the Conqueror and his successors were. We still have the two Houses of Parliament. In the Lords the Chancellor sits on the Woolsack, a reminder of the great medieval industry; and in the Commons M.P.s grant taxes just as knights and burgesses did long ago. Our local government of councils and mayors has its roots in the Middle Ages. And the same is true of the law courts, with their juries of twelve ordinary men and women. Moreover, the judges wear medieval robes and travel round the counties as Henry II's justices did 800 years ago.

The people of modern Britain can create electricity from nuclear energy, feed their problems to computers and fly the Atlantic faster than Chaucer's pilgrims could ride to Canterbury. But they have kept their medieval traditions in law and government – and they are proud to have them. When a foreign tourist comes to Britain, these are the things he is most eager to see.

More about the later Middle Ages

Books

D. Taylor, *Chaucer's England* (Dennis Dobson).

Caxton and the Early Printers (Cape, History Jackdaw series, no. 46).

R. W. Thomson, *How Christianity Grew in England* (Religious Education Press). Chapter 3 for John Wycliffe.

The Canterbury Tales, Geoffrey Chaucer. Look at a copy in the original, to see how English was written in the fourteenth century.

Filmstrips

William Caxton (Visual Information Service). Includes some frames on English social life in the fifteenth century.

Medieval Britain–3: *The Fifteenth Century* (Visual Publications, *People of Other Days*).

Visit

The Public Record Office, London W.C.2, for the earliest examples of English printing. (Also many other documents from the Middle Ages.)

To write and find out

1 Make a list of all the things that would be different about our way of life today if there were no printing presses.

2 How might a bishop have attempted to answer each of John Wycliffe's criticisms of the Church and its teachings?

3 (a) Why do you think people from countries such as the United States and Australia are so interested to see Britain's medieval customs and traditions?

  (b) Make a list of *ten* places to show a foreign visitor interested in our medieval history.

  (c) Some people say the monarchy and all the centuries-old customs in law and government are a waste of time. Do you agree? (Remember to give reasons for your views.)

4 *Either* find out which European countries were the last to free peasants from labour services, *or* find out the countries (some outside Europe) where the Roman Catholic Church is strongest today. How has it changed since the Middle Ages?

Index

Roman law 38
Romans 3–4, 7, 10–11, 36–9
Rome 10, 11, 14–15, 36, 37, 50, 71
Romney 176
Rouen 119, 184
Runnymede 126
Russia 57
Ruthwell Cross 22

St Albans 171–2
'St Louis', see Louis IX
St Peter's Church, Rome 52, 53
Saladin, Sultan 118–9
Salisbury 127, 158
Salisbury Plain 61
Sandwich 176
Santa Sophia, church of 38
Saracens 114–6, 118–21, 193
Savoy Palace 169
Saxony 50–1, 53
Schools, see Education
Scone, Stone of 149
Scotland 7, 21, 57, 69, 144, 147–51
Scots 5, 21, 69
Scunthorpe 62
Scutage 107, 124, 127, 191
Seine, river 59, 62
Selwood, Forest of 60
Senlac Hill 77
Severn, river 7
Sheep farming 192
Sheppey, Isle of 59
Shetland Islands 57
Ships 1–3, 6–7, 56–7, 62, 162
Shires 69
Shops 154
Shrines 111, 142
Sicily 36, 44, 121, 166
Simeon, St 11
Simon de Montfort 128, 130
Sluys, battle of 176–7
Smithfield 170
Snowdonia 145–6
Southampton 70, 163, 175
Spain 15, 37, 38, 43, 44, 50, 142, 166
Squires 89

Stamford 125, 160
Stamford Bridge, battle of 76
Stephen, King 106, 107
Stephen Langton, Archbishop 125
Stewards 100
Stirling, battle of 149
Stirling Castle 149, 150
Stroud 160
Subiaco 11
Sudbury, Archbishop Simon 170
Surrey, Earl of 149
Sussex 69, 76, 181
Sutton Hoo 1·3, 17, 27, 57
Swedes 57
Swein 'Forkbeard' 71
Syria 40, 43, 114, 116

Taverns, see Ale-houses
Templars, see Knights of the Temple
Tenants-in-Chief 86–8
Thames, river 6, 29, 62, 126, 130, 153, 169
Thanes 28, 31, 34, 89, 90
Thanet, Isle of 6, 17, 70
Theobald, Archbishop 108, 110
Theodora, Empress 36
Theodore, Archbishop 21–2, 24
Theodoric 11
Thralls 30, 32
Thunor 17
Tithes 133
Tiw 17
Tonsures 20
Tostig 76
Tournaments 179
Tours 49
Tours, battle of 47
Tower of London 86, 169, 170
Town councils 155–6
Towns 7, 8, 62, 70, 152–60, 191–2
Trade 35, 44, 70, 159–64, 186
Trial by ordeal 34, 109
Troyes, Treaty of 182
Turks, see Saracens
Tweed, river 69
Tyler, Wat 169–70

Under-tenants, see Knights

Universities 139
Urban II, Pope 114

Vandals 36
Venice 119, 163
Verdun, Treaty of 52
Vikings 53, 55–63, 67, 69, 70–2, 83
Villages 7, 34–5, 94–105, 167, 192
Villeins 90, 95–100, 104–5, 165, 167–8, 192
Vinland 58
Vortigern 6

Wales 7, 8, 21, 29, 88, 144–7
Wallace, William 149
Wallingford 70, 80
Waltham 171
Walworth, William 170
Wareham 60
Wash, the 6
Watling Street 62
Wayside crosses 22
Wearmouth 22, 24
Welsh 6, see also Wales
Wergeld 32–3, 62
Wessex 8, 30, 33, 59–62, 67, 69, 70, 72
Westminster Abbey 80, 150, 193
Whitby, Synod of 20–1
White Monks, see Cistercians
White Ship disaster 106
Wilfred, St 21
William I ('the Conqueror') 73–80, 83–91, 110, 145
William II ('Rufus') 91
William fitzOsbern 83
William Marshal 125
Willibrord 22
Winchester 62, 70, 90, 91, 159
Windsor Castle 126
Witan, the 28, 70, 73, 74
Woden 17
Woollen cloth industry 160, 192
Woolsack, the 159, 193
Wool trade 159–60
Wycliffe, John 188–90

York 24, 48, 70, 76, 83, 153, 171